KT-502-861

CHESS FOR CHILDREN

CHESS
FOR CHILDREN

by

R. BOTT & S. MORRISON

With a foreword by
R. G. WADE

Illustrations by
PATRICIA LINDSAY

COLLINS
GLASGOW AND LONDON

This is a first book of chess
suitable for beginners
from 8 to 80

First published in this edition 1968
12th impression 1974
Published by William Collins Sons and Company Limited, Glasgow and London
© 1958 R. Bott and S. Morrison
Printed in Great Britain
ISBN 0 00 106110 0

CONTENTS

ACKNOWLEDGMENTS

In the preparation of this book our thanks are due to all those who have assisted by their criticism and comments. In particular we are indebted to Miss K. Northcroft for her help in checking and preparing the manuscript, to Mr. A. E. Hopkins for the games' records of the London Boys' Championships, and to Mr. B. Reilly—Editor of the British Chess Magazine whose advice has been frequently sought.

Finally may we thank those many teachers and children whose enthusiasm for chess has spurred us on to produce this book, and our respective wives for their enthusiastic encouragement.

FOREWORD

Chess has many qualities to commend it to the young and to their teachers. Through our games we can have revealed to ourselves the positive and negative qualities that constitute our characters, such as courage of convictions, resourcefulness, opportunism, physical endurance, panic, foolishness, thoughtlessness and the ability to survive. Success comes most often as the result of hard work and unflagging concentration. One must keep one step ahead of the opposition.

Chess, like football and athletics, is a recreation to be enjoyed; the game is common to all countries. It is the only game allowed in the Mother of Parliaments; open air sets are to be found in the playgrounds of Milwaukee, U.S.A.; travel long distances by train in Russia and you can obtain a set from the conductor to while away the hours.

Fourteen centuries have passed since chess was evolved from earlier "war" games, and yet no man can truly say that he has become master of the board. With over seventy thousand positions possible after the first two moves by each side and this figure being proportionately increased with each further move, who can see his or her way clearly? Even the most efficient computer cannot cope. Little islands of knowledge have been established with the stretches between full of uncharted shoals to be negotiated. Difficulties have to be faced; the games I enjoy most are ones in which many problems have to be overcome; easy victories give no lasting pleasure.

Nearly all great players learn chess as children and emerge into the international scene in their teens. The present champion of the world, Bobby Fischer, won the national championship of the United States at the age of fourteen. Bobby learnt the moves when he was six. His great rival, Russia's Boris Spassky, played in his first big international event at the age of sixteen. A world championship for those under twenty is held every two years.

The treasures of chess are the many great and beautiful games that have been played, recorded and available in books. *Chess for Children* shows you how to relive your own games. It is written by two London school teachers, who have done much to promote chess among London school children.

R. G. WADE

Blackheath, London
October 1972

INTRODUCTION

Chess has been played for over a thousand years. One of the reasons for its popularity is that chess is an exciting battle game. It was first played in India, and from there travelled across mountains and valleys to the great Persian Empire. The Arabs conquered Persia and in their travels brought the game to the rest of Europe through Spain.

The game used to be considered a pastime for the elderly, but today adult chess players are greatly outnumbered by young players. Indeed, looking at the records of the World Champion Bobby Fischer, the U.S. grandmaster Sammy Reshevsky and British Internationals such as Keene and Jonathan Penrose—and many others—it would appear that you have to start young to be sure of reaching the highest chess standards. You certainly do not have to wait until you are grown up, in order to become a great player.

Thousands of young people compete in school and other tournaments each year and far-sighted chess clubs have thriving junior sections.

It is for the young learner that *Chess for Children* has been written, for the basic principles of the game can be understood by reading the book by yourself. On the other hand, it serves as an instructional book for teachers to use with young beginners.

We hope you enjoy reading it and are stimulated enough to try out the more advanced ideas in our follow-up book, *More Chess for Children*.

R. BOTT
S. MORRISON

The Battlefield

The battlefield is a square chequered board, coloured black and white, with sides eight squares wide, sixty-four squares in all. Have a care when you start, and make sure there is a white square in the right-hand corner.

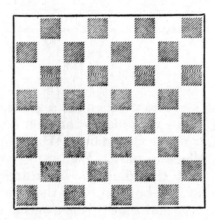

(1) White square in right-hand corner.

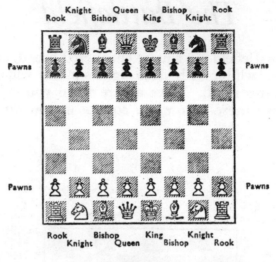

(2) This is the starting position for a game. It is useful to remember that each Queen starts on a square of its own colour, i.e. White Queen on a White square, Black Queen on a Black square. We want you to notice particularly, that this diagram is arranged with the White pieces at the bottom, and the Black pieces at the top. You will find that this is usual in chess books. Therefore all the diagrams in this book will keep to this rule.

Our chessboard is a battlefield. There is going to be a battle between the White Army and the Black Army. Often the fight will end when either the Black King or the White King is defeated. Before that happens, the men will defend their King with all their might. As you will see, they are ready for anything.

THE BATTLEFIELD

We are going to learn how to name different parts of the battlefield.

Eight ranks

(3) These rows of squares are called RANKS.

Eight files

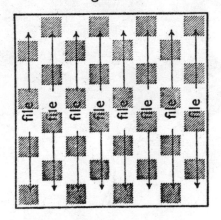

(4) These rows of squares are called FILES.

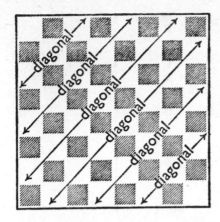

(5) These slanting rows of white squares are called DIAGONALS.

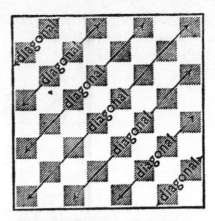

(6) Similarly these slanting rows of black squares are called DIAGONALS.

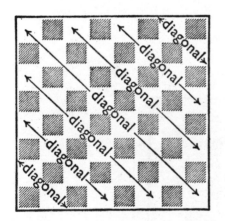

(7) These are white diagonals sloping the other way.

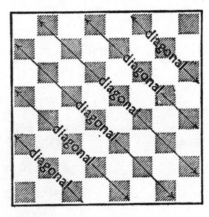

(8) These are black diagonals sloping the other way.

Look again at the starting positions of the two Kings
and the two Queens.

(9)

(10)

The Chessmen

KING

Many centuries ago Kings led their armies into battle. What a fine sight a King made in his glittering armour, with flashing sword and brightly coloured steed. But what an easy target he made! Later Kings became wiser and stayed at home while battles were fought. The King is the man the enemy is after. Although he may move in any direction, he may only move *one* square at a time. Thus he must be strongly defended by his pieces.

NOTE : *In answering the Quiz questions in this section, it will help if you show the squares to which the various pieces may move by using pieces of paper or counters on your chessboard.*

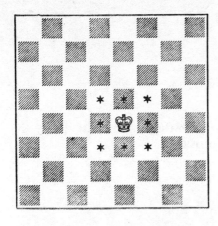

(11) In this position the King may move to any of the eight squares marked *.

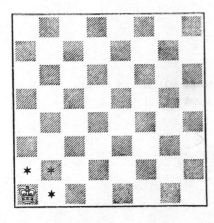

(12) In this position the King may move to any of the three squares marked *.

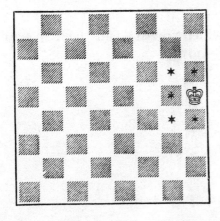

(13) In this position the King may move to any of the five squares marked *.

19

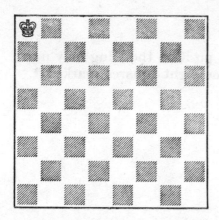

(*Q.* 1) To which squares can the King go on his next move ?

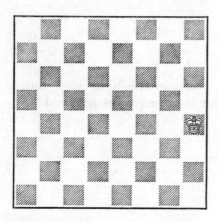

(*Q.* 2) To which squares can the King go on his next move ?

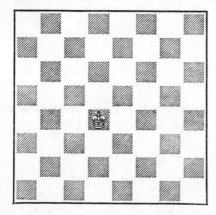

(*Q.* 3) To which squares can the King go on his next move ?

Answers to 'King' Quiz on page 166

 # PAWN

Foot soldiers who never retreat! What General would not give his right arm for such an army? One Pawn may turn the tide of battle, changing likely defeat into victory.

The Pawn moves straight forward along the row or *file* as it is called, on which it starts. It may never move backwards. For its first move it may move either *two* squares forward or *one* square forward along the file, whichever it wishes to do. After the first move, it may move only *one* square forward along the file. If a Pawn reaches the last square on the other side of the board, it must be changed into any other piece except a King. It can be changed into a Knight, a Bishop, a Rook or a Queen. As the Queen is the most powerful piece on the board, it is nearly always best to change such a Pawn into a Queen.

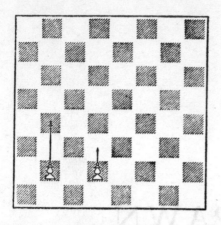

(14) First move—two squares or one square forward as shown.

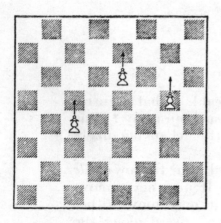

(15) Afterwards only *one* square at a time, as shown in these three examples of Pawn moves.

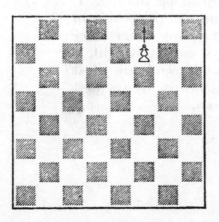

(16) This Pawn, in moving to the last square on its file, must be changed into any piece except a King. This kind of move is known as *Queening the Pawn*, even if the Pawn is changed into a Rook, Bishop or Knight.

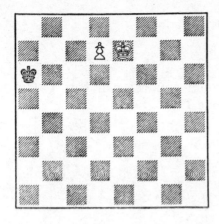

(17) White's **Pawn** is about to become a Queen.

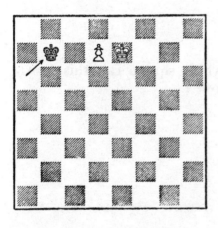

(18) The Black King moves.

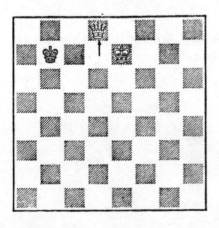

(19) White's turn now. The White Pawn moves to the last square on its file and becomes a Queen.

(*Q*. 4) To which squares can this Pawn go in one move ?

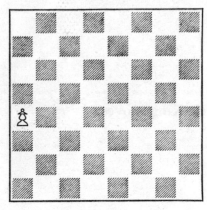

(*Q*. 5) To which square can this Pawn go in one move ?

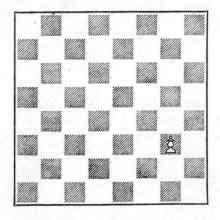

(*Q*. 6) To which square can this Pawn go in one move ?

Answers to 'Pawn' Quiz on page 167

KNIGHT

The gallant Knight brings many an anxious moment to his enemies. His courage is such that he will try anything. You can never be sure where he will strike next. His presence is enough to chill the heart of the enemy.

The Knight is the only piece on the chessboard which can jump over the others. He may jump over friend or foe. If ever an enemy Knight lands where you did not expect him, do not worry too much— the same thing has happened to world champions!

The Knight turns a corner when he moves. He moves in the shape of a capital L, although the L may be upside down or sideways:

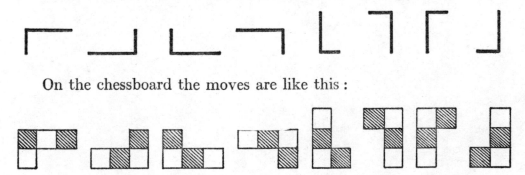

On the chessboard the moves are like this :

The Knight may move from one end of the shape to the other.

25

In other words the Knight moves :

One square along and then *two* sideways
OR
Two squares along and then *one* sideways

If it moves from a Black square it lands on a White square. If it moves from a White square it lands on a Black square. There are two Black Knights and two White Knights. Look back to page 12 and you will see that of White's two Knights, one starts on a White square and the other starts on a Black square. So it is with Black's two Knights.

The Knight is worth 3 Pawns

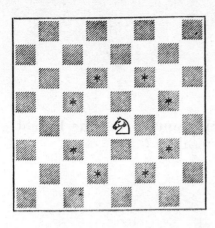

(20) A Knight near the centre of the board attacks or may move to eight squares, like this one.

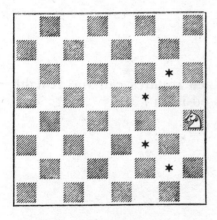

(21) This Knight at the side of the board can move to only four squares.

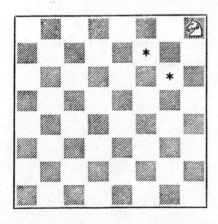

(22) A Knight in the corner, like this one, can move to only two squares. You will see, therefore, that a Knight in the centre is generally much more powerful.

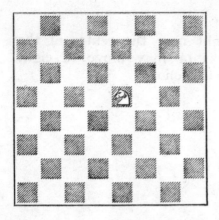

(*Q.* 7) To which squares can the Knight move in this position ?

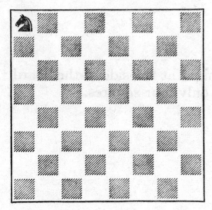

(*Q.* 8) To which squares can the Knight move in this position ?

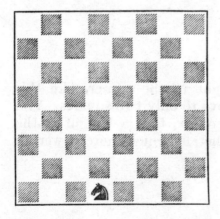

(*Q.* 9) To which squares can the Knight move in this position ?

Answers to 'Knight' Quiz on page 168

BISHOP

The Bishop moves diagonally. Put two Bishops in the middle of the board and the pattern of the squares they attack and can move to is shaped like a cross (see diagram 25). On page **12** you will notice that just as there are four Knights, there are four Bishops. White has two Bishops, one which works only on the White squares and another which works only on the Black squares. In the same way Black has two Bishops, one working on White squares and the other on Black squares.

The Bishop is worth 3 Pawns

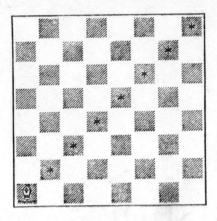

(23) This Bishop attacks or may move to any of the squares along this diagonal marked *.

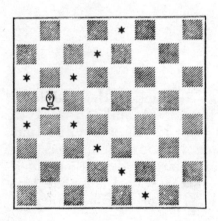

(24) This Bishop attacks or may move to any of the squares along the two diagonals marked *.

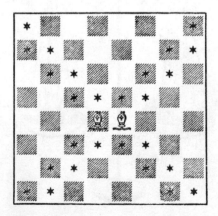

(25) The pattern of squares that these Bishops attack or may move to is shaped like a cross.

From a centre square a Bishop commands 13 other squares while from the side of the chessboard it commands only 7.

30

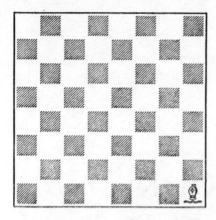

(*Q.* 10) To which squares can this Bishop move in this position ?

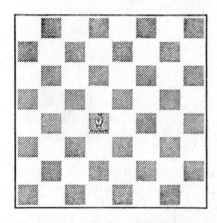

(*Q.* 11) To which squares can this Bishop move in this position ?

(*Q.* 12) To which squares can this Bishop move in this position ?

Answers to ' Bishop' Quiz on page 169

ROOK

The name of this piece comes from the Persian word 'rukh'— which means chariot. Given a clear path, this Rook can crush any enemy soldier under its iron bound wheels. It is sometimes called a Castle. Yes, it looks like one, doesn't it?

The Rook moves to any square along the rank or file it stands on. If you look back to page 12 you will see that there are altogether four Rooks on the board at the beginning of the game. White has two and Black has two. The Rook is the second strongest piece on the board.

The Rook is worth 5 Pawns

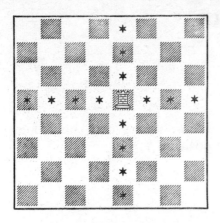

(26) This Rook may move to any square along one rank and one file as shown.

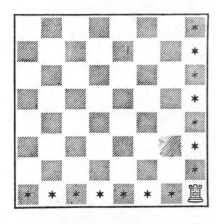

(27) The squares this Rook may move to are again along one rank and one file.

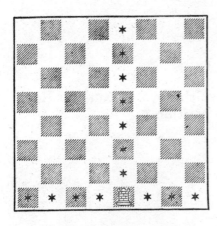

(28) A further example.

A Rook is generally more powerful when placed on a file on which there are no Pawns. This is known as an open file.

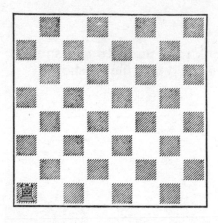

(*Q.* 13) To which squares can the Rook move in this position?

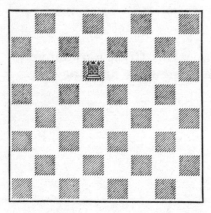

(*Q.* 14) To which squares can the Rook move in this position?

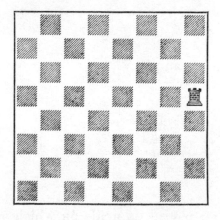

(*Q.* 15) To which squares can the Rook move in this position?

Answers to 'Rook' Quiz on page 170

QUEEN

The Queen is the most powerful piece on the field! What—a soldier Queen you say? Well, Boadicea was a Queen and won battles against the mighty Roman armies, didn't she?

The Queen is the strongest piece on the chessboard. If your Queen is captured you are often in real trouble. The Queen can attack and move like a Rook and also like a Bishop. Put her in the middle of the chessboard and the squares which she attacks look rather like a Union Jack pattern. (See diagram 29).

The Queen is worth 9 Pawns

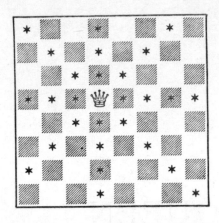

(29) In one move the Queen may go to any square marked *.

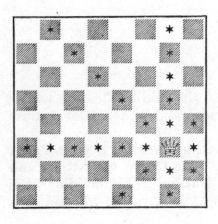

(30) Here the Queen is shown in another position.

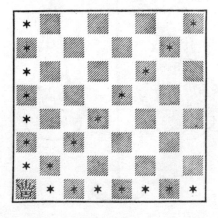

(31) Notice how the Queen attacks like a Rook or Bishop.

36

(*Q.* 16) To which squares can the Queen move in this position ?

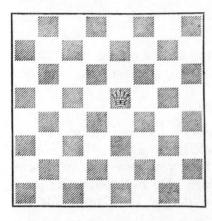

(*Q.* 17) To which squares can the Queen move in this position ?

(*Q.* 18) To which squares can the Queen move in this position ?

Answers to 'Queen' Quiz on page 171

Moving

We are going to find out how you can move your pieces so that you can attack and capture some of your enemy. In a game of conkers you take it in turns to "whack." So you do in chess. In conkers some "whacks" are more damaging than others. One blow might be very slight but the next a shattering one. Chess is very much like this. One move may be a weak one and the next most powerful. You must await your turn to move and when you do have your go make sure that you do the very best you can.

Here are three simple rules for you :

1. White moves first at the beginning of the game.
2. White and Black take it in turns to move, making one move at a time.
3. *One* piece on *one* square at a time.

When you have decided upon your move, make it boldly. If you pick up a piece, then put it down, then pick it up again, then hold it for a couple of minutes, it is perfectly clear that you were not quite sure of your move when you first touched the piece. Do not touch the piece UNTIL YOU ARE SURE ! Then move it confidently (and hope for the best).

TOUCHING AND MOVING

If you touch one of your own Pawns or pieces you MUST move it (unless, of course, it is illegal). There are other rules about touching pieces in the official rules but this is a most important one. (*See page* 164).

ADJUSTING

If, in some way, a piece or Pawn is disturbed accidentally, you may want to adjust its position on its square. When you do this, you must first warn your opponent what you are going to do. Some players use the French expression—" J'adoube." If you fail to give a warning your opponent may insist that you move the piece you touched.

Here is an example of how players take turns in moving.

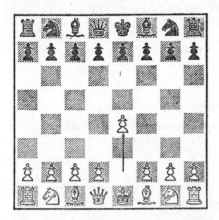

(32) The first move is always by White. He moves a Pawn.

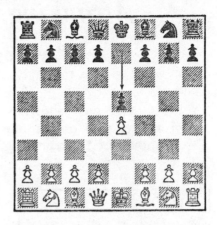

(33) It is now Black's move. He also moves a Pawn.

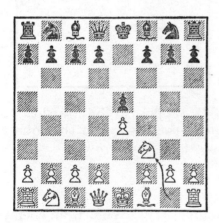

(34) It is White's turn again. He moves a Knight.

(35) Black's turn. He also moves a Knight.

Attacking and Capturing

WITH PIECES

We have shown you that when it is your turn to move, you may move the various pieces to squares shown by * in the diagrams.

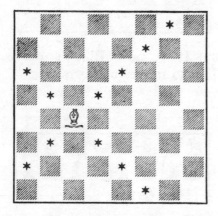

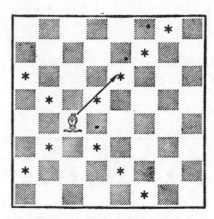

(36) Here is a White Bishop—it may move as shown.

(37) Suppose White wishes to move the Bishop to the square shown by the arrow.

It may move there of course! But you may say "What if an enemy piece already occupies that square?" The answer is simple. It captures the enemy piece, the White Bishop standing in its place. Captured pieces are removed from the board for the rest of the game.

This is how it is done. Here is the board again, only this time there is an enemy Knight on a square to which the Bishop can move. It blocks the path of the Bishop.

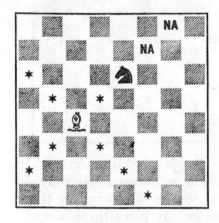

(38) The squares marked NA are no longer attacked by the Bishop. We say the White Bishop is ATTACKING the Black Knight and may capture it if it is White's turn to move.

(39) It is White's turn to move.

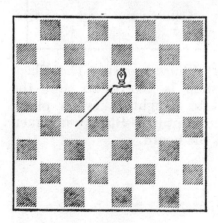

(40) The Bishop moves. It CAPTURES the Knight and stands in its place. The captured Knight is removed from the board for the rest of the game.

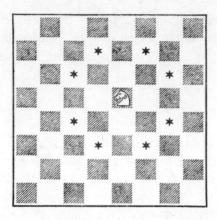

(41) This Knight attacks the squares marked *.

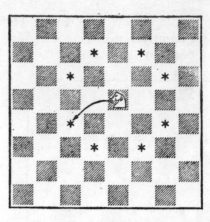

(42) Suppose White wishes to move it as shown. He may do so of course. But suppose there is an enemy piece there already —a Bishop! (See diagram 43).

(43) The Knight is attacking the Bishop. It is White's turn to move.

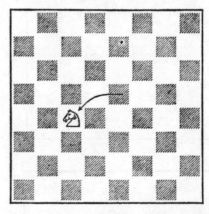

(44) White moves. The Black Bishop is CAPTURED and the White Knight takes its place. The captured Bishop is taken off the board.

Here is an another example of CAPTURING.

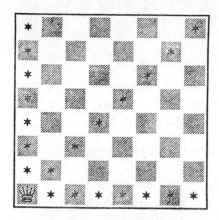

(45) There is a Black Queen in the corner square.

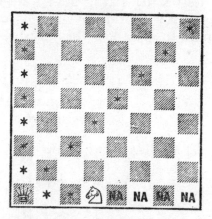

(46) We will suppose that there is a White Knight on a square as shown. You will see the squares marked **NA** are no longer attacked by the Queen as the Knight has blocked the way. We say the Queen attacks the Knight.

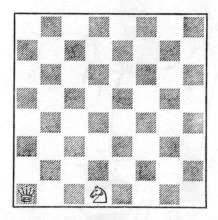

(47) It is Black's turn to move.

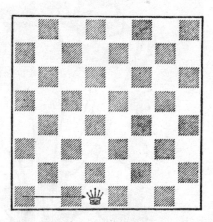

(48) Black moves. The Queen CAPTURES the enemy Knight and stands in its place.

Every chess piece, including the King, may make captures on the chessboard. Pawns have a special attacking and capturing move. They can only capture by moving one square forward diagonally. We have more to say about this on pages 61 to 65.

>If you capture a Queen, it is worth 9 Pawns.
>If you capture a Rook, it is worth 5 Pawns.
>If you capture a Bishop, it is worth 3 Pawns.
>If you capture a Knight, it is worth 3 Pawns.

This tells you, when pieces are captured, how much you have won or lost.

It should be noted that this guide to the value of the various pieces is only a rough measure. Sometimes in a game a Knight or even a Pawn may be more valuable than a Queen.

(*Q.* 19) Which piece can the Queen capture next move ?

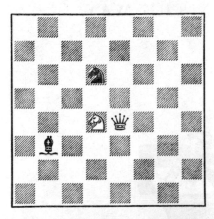

(*Q.* 20) The White Knight can capture one of these Black pieces on its next move. Which one ?

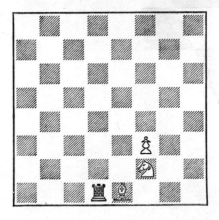

(*Q.* 21) Say which piece this Rook is attacking.

Answers to ' Capturing ' Quiz on page 172

Defending

1—MOVING AWAY

2—DEFENDING AN ATTACKED PIECE

3—CAPTURING THE ATTACKER

4—MOVING A PIECE IN THE WAY

(49) Let us suppose there is a White Bishop together with an enemy Queen on the board as shown.

It is Black's turn to move.

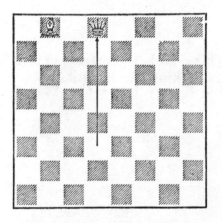

(50) The Black Queen moves. Ouch! The Queen now ATTACKS the poor Bishop. Thank goodness it is White's turn to move. The Bishop must move to a square NOT ATTACKED by the enemy Queen.

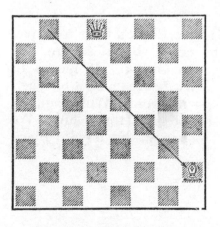

(51) The White Bishop moves to safety. This square will do, although there are many other safe squares.

The Bishop is safe—for the moment.

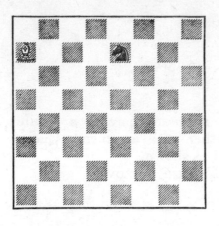

(52) Here is another example. On the board are a White Bishop and a Black Knight. It is White's turn to move.

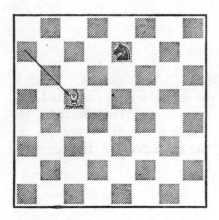

(53) The White Bishop moves. Look out! He is attacking the Knight.

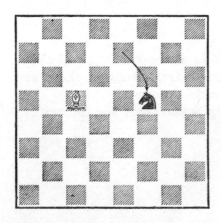

(54) As it is now Black's turn to move, the Knight moves to a square not attacked by the Bishop. It moves to safety, and Black heaves a sigh of relief. The Knight is now on a White square, and the Bishop cannot touch him. We can see this Bishop moves only on Black squares.

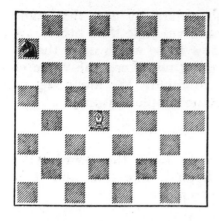

(*Q.* 22) The Knight is attacked. To which squares can it escape ?

(*Q.* 23) The King attacks the Bishop. Which are its escape squares ?

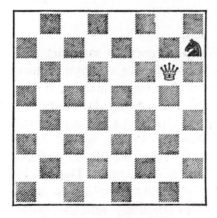

(*Q.* 24) Is the Knight trapped, or is there an escape square ?

Answers to 'Moving Away from Attack' Quiz on page 173

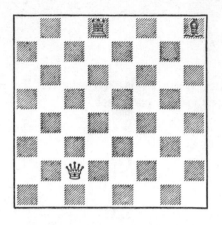

You will realise by now that some pieces are more valuable than others. A Queen we know to be worth more than a Rook. We must now keep the value of these pieces in mind. We are going to have to do some simple Arithmetic.

(55) Suppose we have the board with several pieces on it like this, and it is White's turn to move.

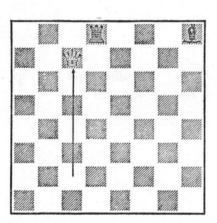

(56) White moves and ATTACKS the enemy Rook. There is another way of avoiding capture as well as by moving away. Black can move his Bishop so that it protects the square on which the Rook stands. We cannot say the Bishop attacks the Rook, because they are both the same colour. We say instead that the Bishop defends the Rook.

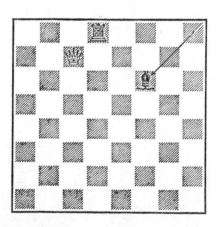

(57) The Bishop moves to support the Rook. It is now White's move again. Can you see what would happen if the Queen captured the enemy Rook now? On his next move the Black Bishop would capture the Queen. White would have given away a Queen (worth 9 pawns) for a Rook (worth 5 pawns). Definitely not worth it. So the Rook has been defended by the Bishop, and is quite safe.

Here is another example of an attacked piece being DEFENDED.

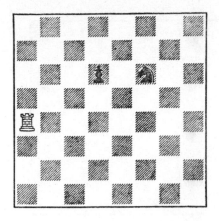

(58) It is White's turn to move.

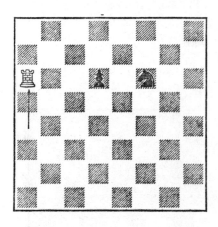

(59) White moves his Rook to ATTACK the little Pawn.
The Pawn is in peril !
But wait ! It can be defended by moving the Knight.

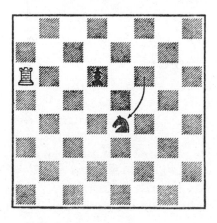

(60) SAFE .
The Pawn is safe. It is DEFENDED. The enemy Rook may capture the Pawn if it wishes, because it is White's move now. But it will not be worth his while. If he captures the Pawn, the Black Knight can capture the Rook. As the Rook is worth 5 Pawns, it is not worth taking the Pawn.

51

Here is a further example :

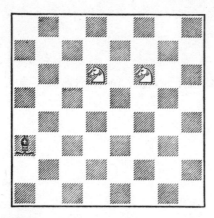

(61) A Black Bishop attacks a Knight, and it is White's turn to move.

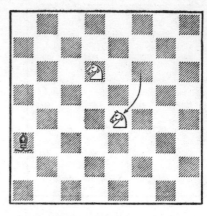

(62) White moves the other Knight to defend the ' attacked ' Knight.

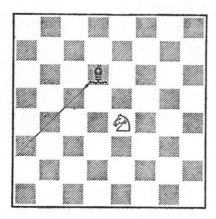

(63) It is Black's turn to move. He captures the Knight. The Knight, being captured, is removed and the Bishop occupies its square. Now it is White's turn to move.

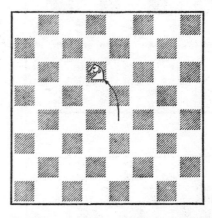

(64) The White Knight, which defended the other White Knight, now captures the Bishop. What is the result ? White has lost a Knight (worth 3 Pawns), Black has lost a Bishop (worth 3 Pawns). The exchange is equal.

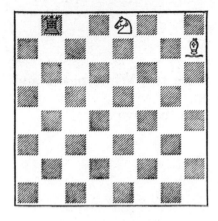

(*Q.* 25) The Black Rook attacks the Knight. Suggest a move to defend this Knight.

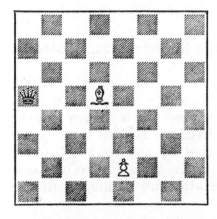

(*Q.* 26) The Black Queen attacks the Bishop. Can this Bishop be defended?

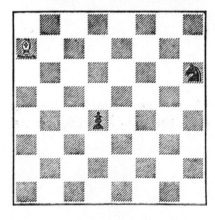

(*Q.* 27) How can the Black Knight defend the attacked Pawn?

Answers to 'Defending the Attacked Piece' Quiz on page 174.

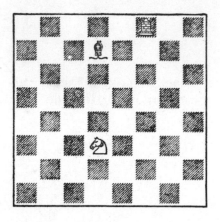

(65) Here you see two White pieces and a Black Bishop.
It is Black's turn to move.

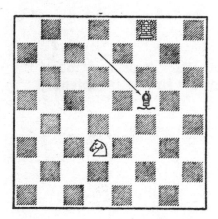

(66) The Black Bishop moves. It attacks the Knight.
It is White's turn to move. The White Knight could move away to a safe square. But there is a better move. Black has moved his Bishop to a square that is attacked by the Rook. Instead of moving the Knight away, White can CAPTURE the attacking Bishop with the Rook.

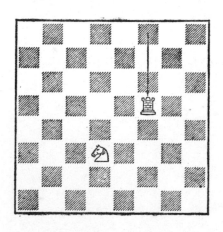

(67) The Rook moves. Black's Bishop is captured and the Rook occupies its square.

(68) Look at this position. Black sees that White's Knight is not defended.

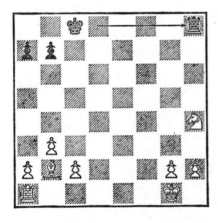

(69) Black moves his Rook to attack the White Knight. He does not notice White's Bishop on the long diagonal attacking him.

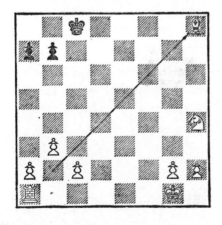

(70) White captures the Black Rook. Black was careless, and pays the penalty.

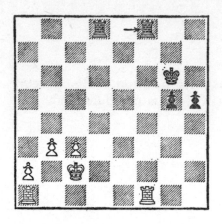

(71) Another example. Black has just moved his Rook to attack the White Rook.

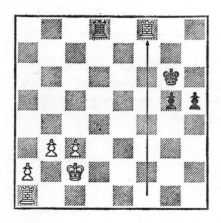

(72) The White Rook captures the attacker.

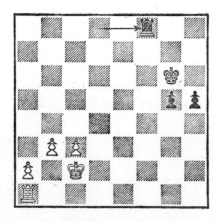

(73) Black recaptures by removing the White Rook with the other Black Rook. Both have given up a Rook. The exchange is equal.

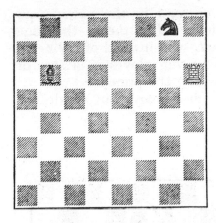

(*Q.* 28) Black to move.
The White Rook is attacking the Black Bishop.
Can Black capture this Rook ?

(*Q.* 29) White to move.
The Black Queen attacks both the White Rook and Bishop.
Can the attacking Queen be captured ?

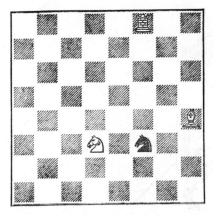

(*Q.* 30). White to move.
The Black Knight attacks the White Bishop.
Can this attacking Knight be captured ?

Answers to 'Capturing the Attacker' Quiz on page 175.

Sometimes you hear on the wireless, or read in the newspapers about a boxer who 'took a blow on his glove.' This means that one opponent has aimed a fierce blow at the other, who instead of trying to dodge out of the way, has used one of his boxing gloves as a sort of shield to soften the blow. This is called blocking the punch.

We can use this idea of *blocking* on the chessboard, but we do not want boxing gloves, please !

Suppose we have this position :

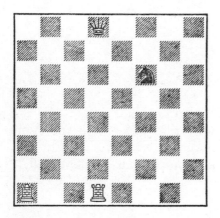

(74) White attacks the Black Queen with a Rook.

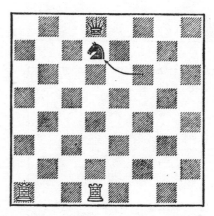

(75) Black moves the Knight in the way, protecting the Queen from attack.

Here is another example :

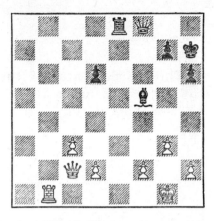

(76) A Black Bishop is attacking the White Queen.

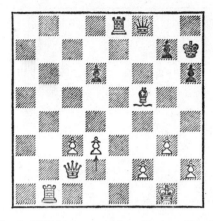

(77) White avoids the attack by moving his Pawn in the way.

In this example a Knight is used to block the attack.

(78) White has attacked the Black Queen with his Rook. The Black Queen has no square to which it can escape, nor can Black capture the attacking Rook without loss.

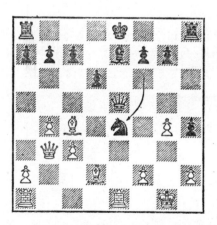

(79) Black makes his best reply, by moving his Knight to block the file between the White Rook and the Black Queen.

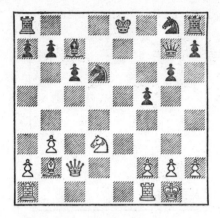

(Q. 31) The White Bishop attacks the Black Queen. Can Black move a piece in the way to block this attack?

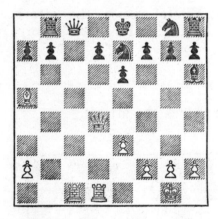

(Q. 32) The Black Queen is attacked by the White Rook.
Can Black block this attack?

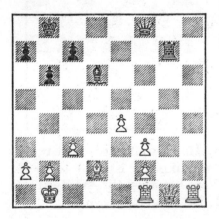

(Q. 33) White's Queen is attacked by the Black Rook. Find a way of blocking this attack.

Answers to 'Moving a Piece in the Way' Quiz on page 176.

Attacking and Capturing

WITH PAWNS

You will remember how Pawns move. They move forward along the files one square at a time except on their first move, when they may move either one square or two squares forward.

> You may think the Pawn is most unusual. So it is !
>
> It cannot be moved backwards—all other pieces can.
>
> It can end its march along the file by becoming a Queen, Rook, Bishop or Knight.

Here is another difference :

> The Pawn has a special move when capturing.
>
> It attacks and CAPTURES *diagonally.*

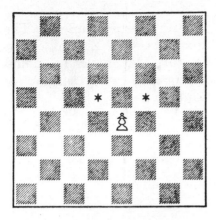

(80) The Pawn attacks one square diagonally forward to the left and right as shown.

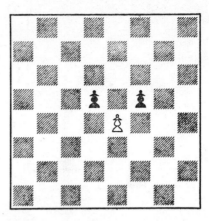

(81) In this diagram two Black Pawns stand on the attacked squares.

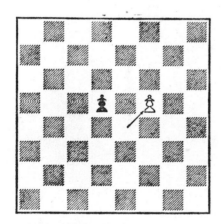

(82) To capture one of the Black Pawns, the White Pawn moves diagonally forward, right or left. The right-hand Pawn is captured in this diagram.

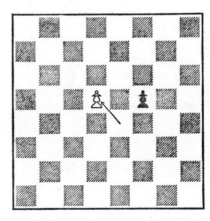

(83) The left-hand Pawn is captured by moving diagonally forward to the left.

(84) Here is another example. The Pawn this time attacks a Knight. If it were White's turn to move he could either move forward one square or capture the Knight.

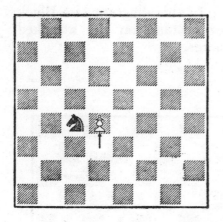

(85) The Pawn has moved forward one square.

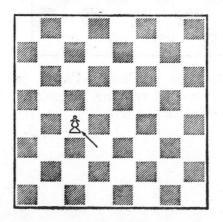

(86) Instead of moving forward, however, he could capture the Knight. In this case he would capture diagonally with his special capturing move like this. The Knight is removed.

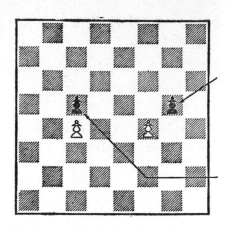

(87) Look at this position. White to move. This Black Pawn can be captured.

This Black Pawn cannot be captured.

Pawns move forward along files when not capturing.

Pawns capture diagonally.

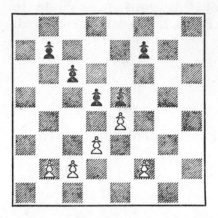

(*Q. 34*) White to move. Can you see a White Pawn which can capture a Black Pawn?

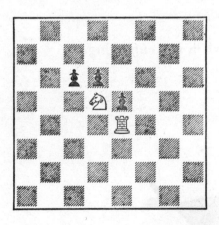

(*Q. 35*) Black to move. Which Black Pawn can capture which White piece?

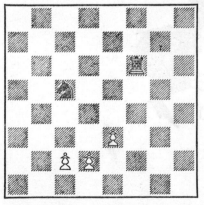

(*Q. 36*) Suggest a White Pawn move which will attack a Black piece.

Answers to 'Attacking and Capturing with Pawns' Quiz on page 177.

Checking

AND GETTING OUT OF CHECK

In chess, although we are always trying to defeat the enemy King and his forces, we do give a warning if we attack the King. How do we do this? You have already learned how one piece can attack another (see diagrams 39, 43 and 47). When a King is attacked you warn your opponent by saying " CHECK." The rules do not require you to say " check," but it is polite and usual to do so. No player is allowed to leave his King attacked, that is to say, in " check." His reply must be to get out of check. Neither must the King put himself in check by occupying an attacked square. It follows that two Kings may never occupy squares that are next to one another.

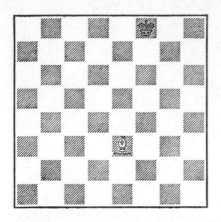

(88) Look at this position. A Black King and a White Bishop are on the board.

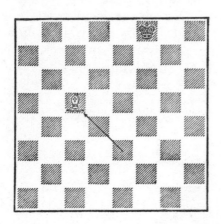

(89) We move the Bishop. It is attacking the King. We say " check."

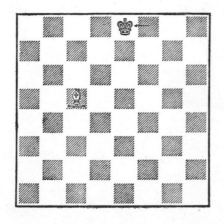

(90) The King must get out of check. The King moves. He is not attacked now. He is no longer in check.

68

Let us look at another example.

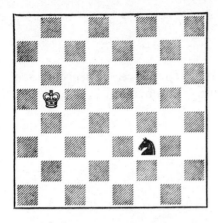

(91) On this board are a White King and a Black Knight.

(92) The Black Knight is moved so that it is attacking the White King. The Black player says " check."

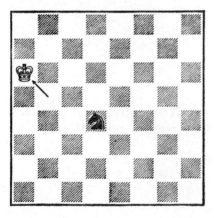

(93) The King gets out of check. He moves to a square not attacked by the Knight.

So you see one way to get out of check is to *move away*.

One more example :

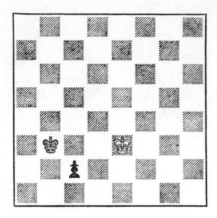

(94) It is Black to move. Can you see how White may be checked ?

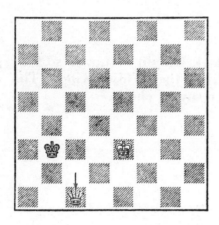

(95) Black moves. His Pawn reaches the end of its file and becomes a Queen. White is now in check.

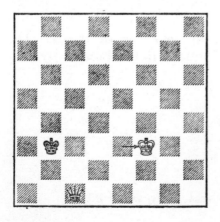

(96) The White King moves out of check by moving to a square not attacked by the Queen.

If any of your pieces are attacked, you can sometimes stop this by capturing the attacker. (See page 54). This gives you a clue to another way of escaping from check. Can you guess what it is?

Answer: Capture the piece which is checking the King.

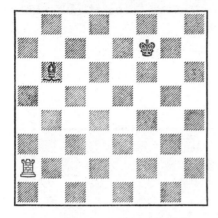

(97) Look at this example. On this board are a Black King and Bishop, and a White Rook.

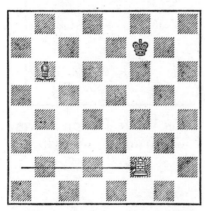

(98) The Rook moves and attacks the King. White says " check." The King must get out of check. He could move away but as the Black Bishop is attacking the Rook he can capture it.

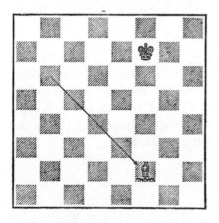

(99) Black moves. The Bishop captures the White Rook and the Black King is no longer in check.

There is yet another way of escaping from check. Do you remember how pieces can be used to " block " the way ? (See pages 58 and 59). A King can sometimes get one of his pieces to help him just like that. A piece can be moved so that the square on which the King is standing is no longer attacked. This piece can be used to " block " the attack. Let us look at some diagrams to see how it is done.

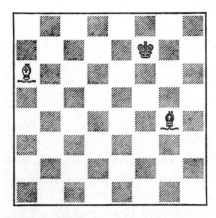

(100) Here is a position with a White Bishop and a Black King and Bishop.

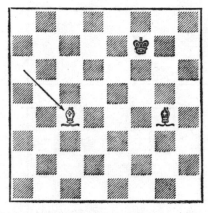

(101) The White Bishop moves. The Black King is in check.

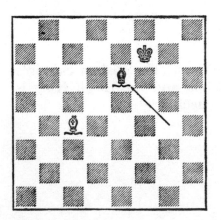

(102) The Black Bishop moves in between the attacking White Bishop and the Black King. The brave Bishop interposes (blocks the way) and defends the King. The King is no longer directly attacked. The King is out of check.

72

Here is another example :

(103) On the board are a White King with a White Queen and Knight nearby, together with a Black Queen.

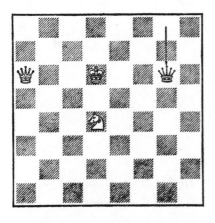

(104) The Black Queen moves and checks the King. The White player can use his Knight to block the rank between his King and the attacking Queen. If the King moves away instead, then the White Queen would be captured.

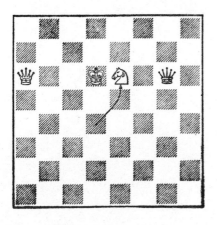

(105) The White Knight moves. The way is now blocked. The White King is no longer in check.

73

Can you remember all the ways of getting out of check ?

Here they are :

1. Moving the King away.

2. Capturing the attacker.

3. Moving a piece in the way.

NOTE : *You cannot move a piece in the way if your King is checked by a Knight. Why not? Because a Knight can jump over pieces.*

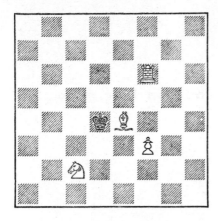

(*Q.* 37) Which White piece is checking the Black King ?

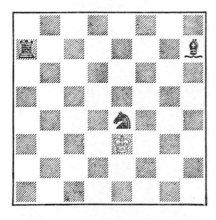

(*Q.* 38) How can a Black piece check the White King in one move ?

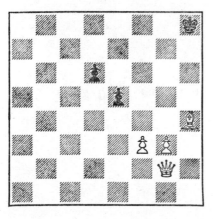

(*Q.* 39) How can a White piece check the Black King in one move ?

Answers to ' Check' Quiz on page 178.

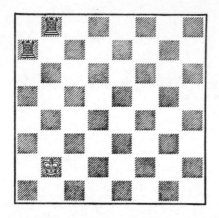

(*Q.* 40) How can this King get out of check ?

(*Q.* 41) How can this King get out of check ?

(*Q.* 42) How can this King get out of check ?

Answers to ' Getting out of Check' Quiz on page 179.

Checkmate

We made an expedition ;
We met a host and quelled it ;
We forced a strong position,
And killed the men who held it. . . .

Fierce warriors rushed to meet us ;
We met them and o'erthrew them :
They struggled hard to beat us ;
But we conquered them, and slew them.

As we drove our prize at leisure,
The King marched forth to catch us :
His rage surpassed all measure,
But his people could not match us.
He fled to his hall-pillars ;
And, ere our force we led off,
Some sacked his house and cellars,
While others cut his head off. . . .

THOMAS PEACOCK

To capture a King is a dangerous and difficult business against a skilful enemy. Think carefully then.

We know how to attack a King. But he may have ways of escape.
Suppose we attacked the King in such a way that our enemy :

1. Could not move the King away.
2. Could not capture the attacker.
3. Could not move a piece in the way.

Can this be done ? Look at the positions on the next page :

77

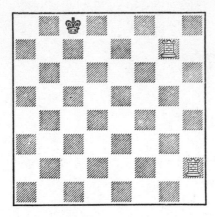

(106) White to move.

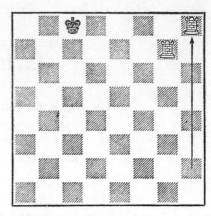

(107) A White Rook moves to attack the Black King. The King cannot get out of check. It is CHECKMATE and White wins the game.

(108) White to move.

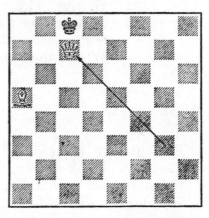

(109) The White Queen moves to attack the Black King. CHECKMATE! The King cannot capture the Queen because it is protected by the Bishop.

If there is no way of getting out of check, it is CHECKMATE. The King is captured—the game is over.

Two more examples :

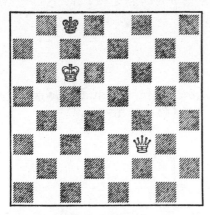

(110) A Black King is about to be caught !

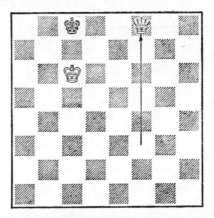

(111) The White Queen moves, attacking the Black King. He cannot move next to the White King. You will remember two Kings may never stand next to each other. It is checkmate.

(112) A White King is about to be captured.

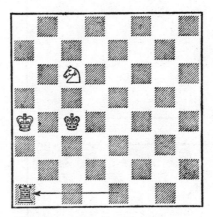

(113) The Black Rook moves, attacking the White King. There is no square to which the King can go. He cannot move out of check. He has a White Knight, but this piece cannot capture the attacker nor move in the way. There is no escape. The King is checkmated.

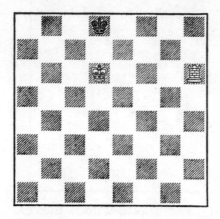

(*Q.* 43) White to move and checkmate the Black King in one move.

(*Q.* 44) Black to move and checkmate the White King in one move.

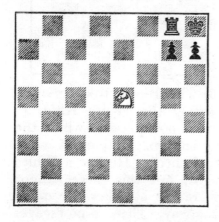

(*Q.* 45) White to move and checkmate the Black King in one move.

Answers to 'Checkmate' Quiz on page 180.

Castling

You will remember that we said earlier that Kings no longer lead their armies into battle. Instead of glory on the battlefield they later preferred safety behind thick castle walls (no one could have blamed them for that).

In chess there is a special move by which the King may tuck himself safely away. This move is called " Castling." In the act or move of castling you move *two* pieces.

The two pieces to be moved are the King and a Rook.

The word " castling " comes from the name of the piece—a castle —which is another name for the Rook.

To castle you move the King two squares towards the Rook you are going to use and the Rook comes round the other side of him. It is a rule that the King is moved first when you castle.

(114) Here we show the King and the King's Rook on their starting squares.

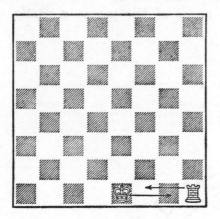

(115) If you want to castle with the King's Rook, the King moves two squares towards this Rook. At the same time the Rook comes round to the other side as shown.

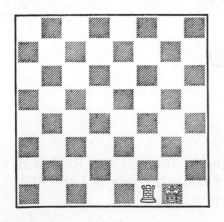

(116) After you have castled on the King's side the King and Rook will be placed like this.

82

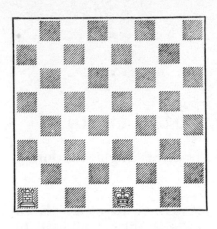

(117) If you want to castle with the Queen's Rook the King moves two squares towards this Rook. At the same time the Rook comes round to the other side.

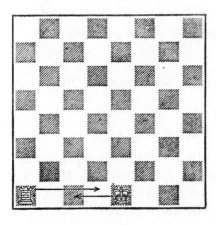

(118) Like this.

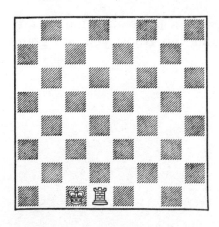

(119) After you have castled on the Queen's side the King and the Rook will be placed like this.

SIX THINGS WHICH STOP YOU CASTLING

Either of the first two cases prevent you from castling at all during the game.

1. Once you have moved your King you cannot castle at all. Even if you have moved him back again, you are still not allowed to castle.

2. Just as you may not castle if the King has moved before, neither may you castle at all if the Rook concerned has previously been moved.

In the following four cases you are prevented from castling only while any of these conditions exist.

3. You are not allowed to castle if your King is in check.

4. You are not allowed to castle if the King lands on a square that is being attacked by the enemy. This would mean that the King would move into check, and this, of course, is not allowed. The King may NEVER move on to an attacked square.

5. You are not allowed to castle if your King has to move across a square that is being attacked.

6. You are not allowed to castle if there is a piece standing on any of the squares between the King and the Rook you are going to use.

Here are some positions to explain what we have just said.

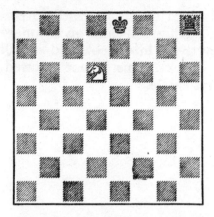

(120) The King is in check by the Knight. In this position Black **cannot** castle.

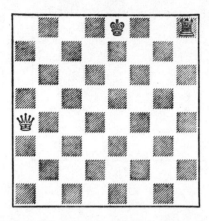

(121) The White Queen checks the King. Again Black cannot castle in this position.

(122) The Black Bishop attacks a square over which the King would have to pass to castle. Another position where White **cannot castle.**

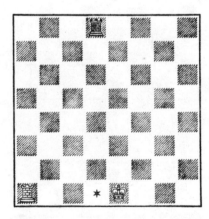

(123) In just the same way, White cannot castle here because the King would have to cross over a square attacked by the Black Rook.

(124) If Black attempts to castle in this position, the King will land on a square attacked by the White Rook and so will move into check. This is not allowed. Black cannot castle.

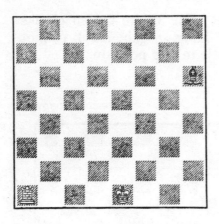

(125) Here the Black Bishop attacks the square on which the White King will land if White attempts to castle. So again White is prevented from castling.

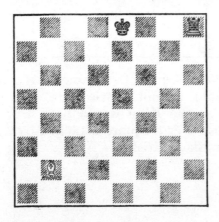

(126) Here you see the Rook is attacked. This, however, does *not* prevent you from castling.

86

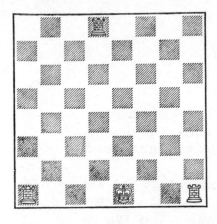

In the following three Quiz questions we will say that neither the two Rooks nor King concerned in castling have moved before.

(*Q.* 46) Can you say on which side White may castle ?

(*Q.* 47) May Black castle on his next move ?

(*Q.* 48) May White castle next move ?

Answers to ' Castling ' Quiz on page 181.

En Passant

Once upon a time you were allowed to move a Pawn only one square on its first move, whereas to-day, as you have learned, you may move an unmoved Pawn two squares.

There is only one more rule to learn before you are able to play a game of chess, and this rule concerns this double-square move of the Pawn. This rule is called the 'en passant' rule. 'En passant' is French for " in passing," so if you did not know any French before, you do now !

After the most careful consideration the authors have come to the conclusion that the e.p. (en passant) rule was introduced by someone simply to make the game more awkward than it already was !

You are White and you have a Pawn which has reached the fifth rank from your side of the board. In front of it are some Black Pawns on their starting squares.

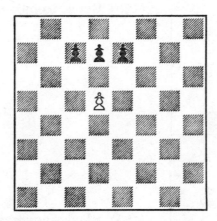

(127) It is Black to move. Black may move either of his two outside Pawns two squares or one square. The middle Pawn may, of course, move only one square. If Black decides to move one of these outside Pawns *two* squares, bringing it to the side of the White Pawn, then White may play a special capturing move.

Here is a similar position:

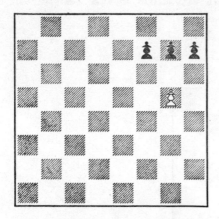

(128) Black to move.

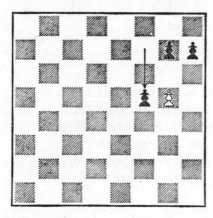

(129) Black moves a Pawn two squares so that it leaps to the side of the White Pawn.

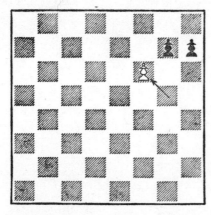

(130) White moves, and captures this Black Pawn just as if it had moved *only one square*.

This is the peculiar ' en passant ' move.

It should be clear that the capturing Pawn must be on the 5th rank, to be in a position to capture en passant.

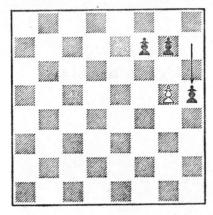

(131) In this position Black moves a Pawn two squares to the side of the White Pawn.

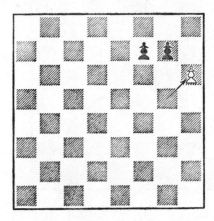

(132) The Black Pawn is captured e.p. and taken off the board for the rest of the game.

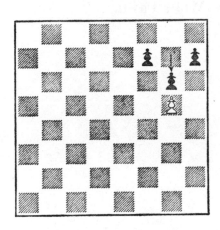

(133) If the middle Black Pawn is moved as shown, no capture e.p. takes place. You may only capture e.p. if your opponent's Pawn moves two squares at once to the side of your pawn.

You may only capture 'en passant' on the NEXT move after your opponent's Pawn has moved to the side of your Pawn. If you do not capture it on the very next move you have lost the chance to do so. You cannot say later on " I'll now capture e.p. the Pawn you moved next to mine six moves ago."

Here are some examples of taking ' en passant ' :

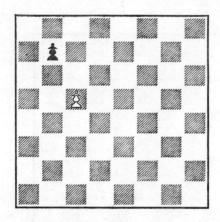

(134) It is Black's turn to move.

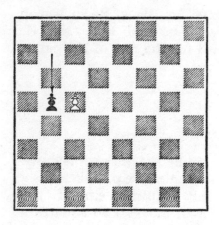

(135) Black moves two squares forward alongside the White Pawn.

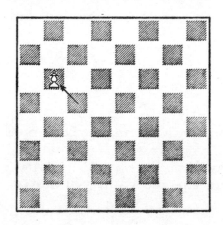

(136) The White Pawn takes ' en passant.'

92

(137) Here is a White Pawn on the fifth rank facing two Black Pawns. One of these two Black Pawns is able to move forward two squares. It is Black's turn to move.

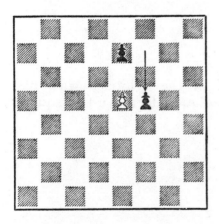

(138) Black moves a Pawn forward two squares alongside the White Pawn.

(139) White replies by capturing 'en passant.'

Here is an example as it would appear on the near side of the board :

(140) It is White's turn to move.

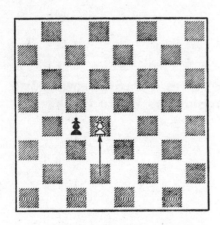

(141) As it is the White Pawn's first move it is allowed to move two squares if it wishes.

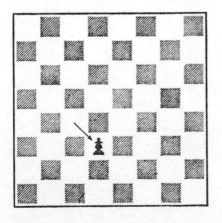

(142) Black replies by capturing 'en passant.'

94

Naturally, you do not have to capture 'en passant' if you do not wish to. You could move your Pawn forward instead or move another piece. Look at this position:

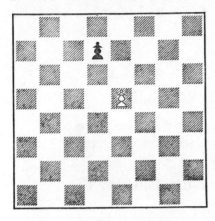

(143) Black to move.

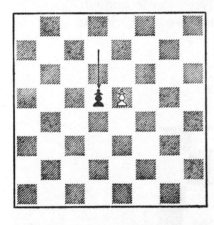

(144) Black moves and now White may capture 'en passant.'

(145) White decides to move on instead.

95

Here are reminders about the ' en passant ' move.

1. The taking Pawn has to be on its fifth rank.

2. The Pawn that is taken has to have moved two squares forward on its first move so that it moves to the side of the taking Pawn.

3. The capturing Pawn moves as if the Pawn to be taken had moved only *one* square.

4. The ' en passant ' move may only be made immediately following the move of the Pawn which can be taken.

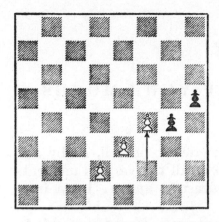

(Q. 49) White has just moved a Pawn two squares as shown by the arrow. Can Black take en passant ?

(Q. 50) White has just moved a Pawn one square as shown by the arrow. Can Black take en passant ?

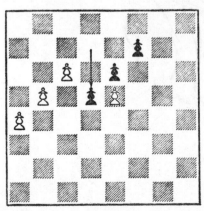

(Q. 51) A Black Pawn has just moved two squares as shown by the arrow. How can White capture en passant ?

Answers to 'En Passant' Quiz on pages 182 and 183.

Notation

HOW TO KEEP A NOTE OF YOUR MOVES

When we play games such as football, cricket, netball, rugby and hockey we have to rely on our memories to recall the various incidents in them. Remembering good play gives pleasure, and we learn from our mistakes.

In chess we do not have to rely solely on memory for it is possible to keep an *exact* record of how a game was played. There are countless thousands of chess games recorded in books, and it is exciting to think that although some of them were played hundreds of years ago, we may play them over again to-day.

To show you six moves in the order in which they were played in a game of chess we *could* show you like this :

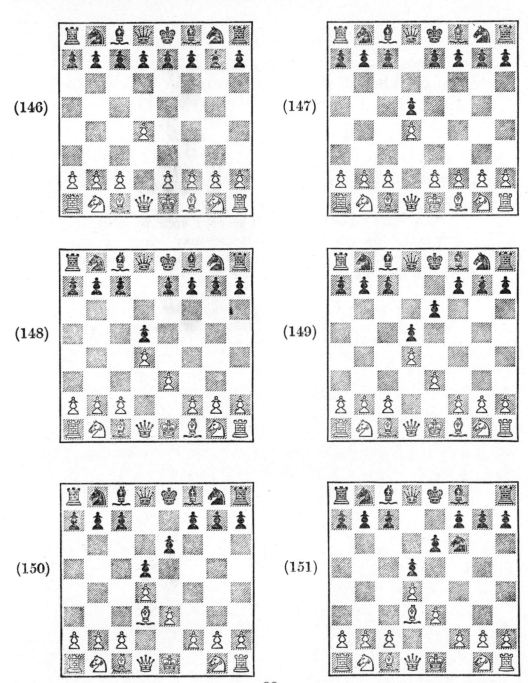

(146)

(147)

(148)

(149)

(150)

(151)

How much easier it would be to write down the moves without taking up all that room. In fact, we can do that. We may write the moves down like this:

	White	*Black*
1.	P—Q4	P—Q4
2.	P—K3	P—K3
3.	B—Q3	Kt—KB3

This is a Chess Code! It is an easy code to master, however, and one which everyone may learn. It is not a secret code (except to those unhappy people who cannot play chess).

All the squares on the chessboard are numbered. By using these numbers, and letters for the pieces, we are able to write down the moves.

Suppose you are White. The square on which the King starts is called K1, the square in front of it K2, etc.

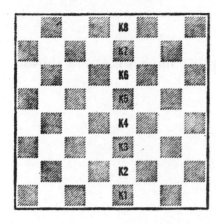

(152) Here you see the King's file marked with these numbers. They start on one side at K1 and go along the file ending on the other side of the board at K8.

Similarly the starting square of the Queen is called Q1, the square in front of that Q2, and so on.

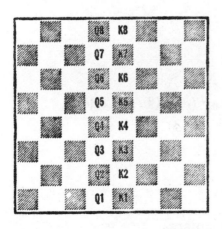

(153) So now you see in this diagram both the King's file and the Queen's file marked.

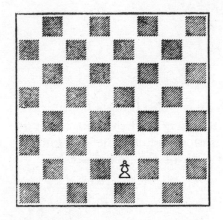

(154) Suppose we have a Pawn as shown.

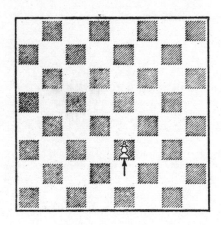

(155) We move it one square forward like this.

If we want to say what move has been made we could say :

" The Pawn on the King's second square has moved to the King's third square."

But we may write it in a short way (our Chess Code) like this :

P—K3

P means Pawn.
— means moves to.
K3 means King's third square.

P—K3 means that the Pawn has moved to square K3.

All the pieces have their special letters.

Here they are :

        K =King
        Q =Queen
        R =Rook
        B =Bishop
        Kt=Knight
        P =Pawn
        × means " takes."

For example :

   P×P stands for " Pawn takes Pawn."
   R×Q stands for " Rook takes Queen."

   O—O means " Castles on the King's side."
   O—O—O means " Castles on the Queen's side."

Here are all White's pieces. We have left out the Pawns for the moment.

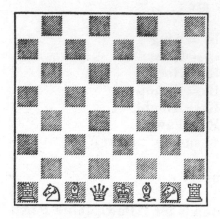

(156) There are two Rooks, two Bishops and two Knights. We know that the Rook may be written —R. But we have *two* Rooks—twins !

How shall we tell them apart ? We shall call the Rook on the King's side of the board—KR (King's Rook), and the Rook on the Queen's side —QR (Queen's Rook).

In the same way we can have —KB (King's Bishop), QB (Queen's Bishop), KKt (King's Knight) and QKt (Queen's Knight).

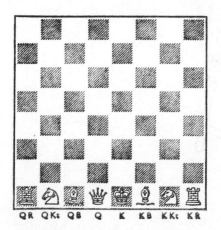

(157) Here you see White's pieces labelled with their appropriate letters.

104

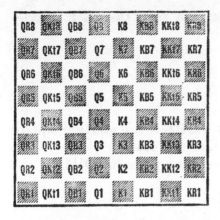

QR8	QKt8	QB8	Q8	K8	KB8	KKt8	KR8
QR7	QKt7	QB7	Q7	K7	KB7	KKt7	KR7
QR6	QKt6	QB6	Q6	K6	KB6	KKt6	KR6
QR5	QKt5	QB5	Q5	K5	KB5	KKt5	KR5
QR4	QKt4	QB4	Q4	K4	KB4	KKt4	KR4
QR3	QKt3	QB3	Q3	K3	KB3	KKt3	KR3
QR2	QKt2	QB2	Q2	K2	KB2	KKt2	KR2
QR1	QKt1	QB1	Q1	K1	KB1	KKt1	KR1

(158) We have shown you that each square can have a number from 1 to 8. Here is the board with all the squares labelled as from *White's* side of the board.

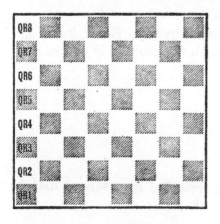

QR8
QR7
QR6
QR5
QR4
QR3
QR2
QR1

(159) After seeing the confusion Will and Bert found themselves in, you will not be surprised when we say that Black must label the squares as well. Look once again at White's Queen's Rook file.

This is where you may find it necessary to turn the book upside-down !

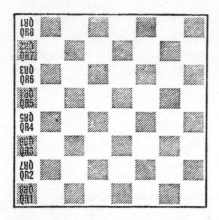

(160) White's QR8 is the starting square for Black's Queen's Rook.

Black calls this square his QR1.

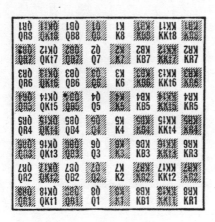

(161) Here is the board fully labelled both from White's point of view and Black's.

So you will see that each square has two labels—a Black label and a White label. Then we shall not be faced with the trouble Will and Bert found themselves in !

On page 107 there is a game that was recorded in a school match. See if you can play it over on your own board.

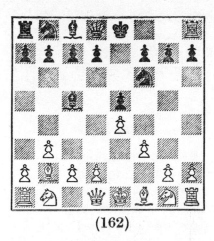

(162)

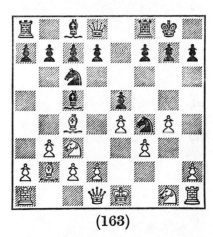

(163)

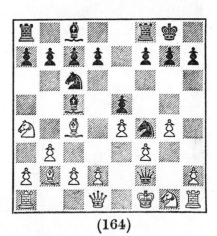

(164)

GAME No. 1

White	*Black*
G. SHORTEN	J. PICKLES
9 *yrs.*	11 *yrs.*
1. P—K4	P—K4
2. P—KB3	B—B4
3. P—QKt3	Kt—KB3
4. B—Kt2	Kt—B3
5. B—B4	O—O
6. Kt—B3	Kt—KR4
7. P—KKt4	Kt—B5
8. Kt—R4	Q—R5 ch.
9. K—B1	Q—B7 mate

NOTE : Look at the notation for Black's second move. It is B—B4. There was no need to say ' *KB—QB4* ' as the Bishop concerned was the only one that could move, and it could only move to one of the two B4 squares. Similarly with White's fourth move B—Kt2. Although the other Bishop can move, it cannot go to a square labelled Kt2. See how many other moves you can find where the *full* notation has not been used. In this chess code you write down the least number of letters needed to describe accurately the move.

(162) Position after White's 4th move B—Kt2.

(163) Position after Black's 7th move . . . . . Kt—B5.

(164) Position after Black's 9th move . . . . . Q—B7 ch. mate.

In the caption (163) you will see before " Kt—B5 " a row of dots. Whenever you see this row of dots in front of the move it means it is a Black move. A move showing no row of dots but giving the number of the move means it is a White move, i.e.

" 4. K—Kt1 " is a White move
" . . . . . B—B4 " is a Black move.

You will notice that in recording games in Notation, the White moves are shown on the left-hand side and the Black moves on the right. If, therefore, you wish to mention a Black move on its own, the row of dots is put in front to make it clear that it is the right-hand column.

Here is another Game to practise notation. It is a record of a game between A. Anderssen and J. Dufresne in Berlin, 1854. Anderssen was regarded as World Champion from 1851 to 1858. The following game is one of the most remarkable on record, and is known as the " Evergreen."

(165) Position after Black's 8th move . . . . . Q—B3.

GAME No. 2

White ANDERSSEN	Black DUFRESNE
1. P—K4	P—K4
2. Kt—KB3	Kt—QB3
3. B—B4	B—B4
4. P—QKt4	B×KtP
5. P—B3	B—R4
6. P—Q4	P×P
7. O—O	P—Q6
8. Q—Kt3	Q—B3

continued on page 109

108

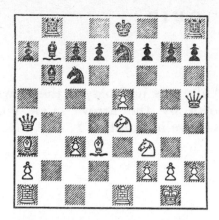

(166) Position after Black's 16th move . . . . . Q—R4.

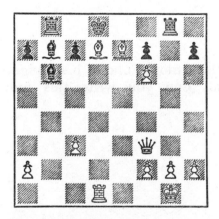

(167) Final position.

continued from page 108

9.	P—K5	Q—Kt3
10.	R—K1	KKt—K2
11.	B—R3	P—Kt4
12.	Q×P	R—QKt1
13.	Q—R4	B—Kt3
14.	QKt—Q2	B—Kt2
15.	Kt—K4	Q—B4
16.	B×QP	Q—R4
17.	Kt—B6 ch.	P×Kt
18.	P×P	R—Kt1
19.	QR—Q1	Q×Kt
20.	R×Kt ch.	Kt×R
21.	Q×P ch.	K×Q
22.	B—B5 ch.	K—K1
23.	B—Q7 ch.	K—Q1
24.	B×Kt mate.	

NOTE: On Black's 10th move you should have moved the Kt which was standing on KKt1. Similarly the Kt which should have been moved on White's 14th move was the one standing on QKt1.

109

(*Q. 52*) White has just played the Pawn move shown by the arrow. Can you write this move in notation?

(*Q. 53*) Black moves one of his Knights, as shown. Can you write this move down?

(*Q. 54*) White has just moved his Rook to the square indicated by the arrow. How would you write this move down?

Answers to 'Notation' Quiz on page 183.

Quiz 55. Look at these two diagrams marked A and B. Read the notes under each and then answer the question under B.

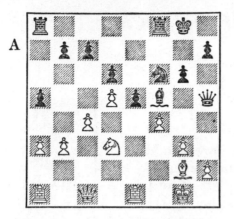 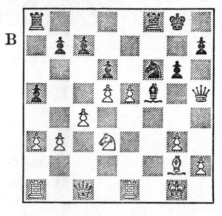

Position in the middle of a game, with White to move.

The same game one move later. Can you find White's move and write it down in notation?

Quiz 56. Again, read the notes under A and B, then answer the question under B.

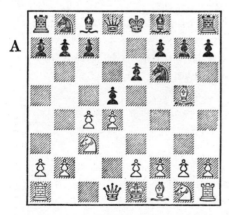 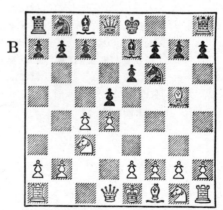

Position in the middle of another game, with Black to move.

Position in the same game one move later. Can you find the move Black has made and write it down?

Answers to 'Notation' Quiz on page 183.

The Double Attack

Did you ever hear tell
  Of Two Gun Pete ?
He'd Pawns for his eyeballs
  And two left feet !

He came across two bandits
  One frosty summer night—
One was to the left of him,
  The other on the right.

We were giving a friend of ours some chess advice. The conversation went like this :

BOTT :	Attack the Queen. You'll be in serious trouble if you don't.
MORRISON :	No, attack the Rook ! You will be checkmated if you don't.
BOTT :	Ridiculous ! Attack the Queen !
MORRISON :	The Rook I say !
TWO GUN PETE :	Do what I did to the bandits, attack them both at once.
BOTT : MORRISON : }	Of course !

If, when you attack an enemy piece other than the enemy King, your opponent does not notice it is in danger, then you are lucky and may capture it on your next move. But if, as is very likely, he moves the piece away or defends it, then he is no longer in trouble and you have to try again. It is, however, possible to make a move which attacks more than one piece AT THE SAME TIME. This kind of attack can be very powerful, as the following examples show.

Look at this position :

(168) It is White's turn to move. If he moves the Knight to Q5 it attacks four Black pieces at once.

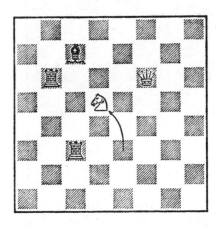

(169) White moves Kt—Q5. The Knight attacks four pieces at once. It is now Black's turn to move.

As he may move only one piece to safety it is clear that White is going to be able to capture one of the other three pieces on his next move.

We have shown you four pieces attacked at once. Although it is possible for this number of pieces to be attacked by one piece, it would be unusual. What *is* common on the chessboard is to find one piece attacking two enemy pieces. That is why this sort of attack is called DOUBLE ATTACK or FORK.

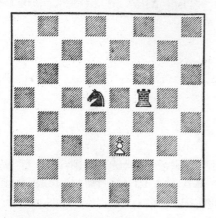

(170) White to move. If the Pawn is moved one square forward it will fork the two Black pieces.

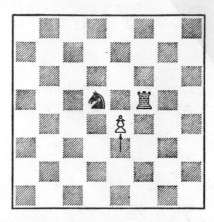

(171) White moves P—K4. The Black Rook and Knight have been forked.

(172) Black moves his Rook to safety.

(173) White captures the Knight, victim of a Pawn fork.

You see, our little Pawn can occasionally wield the most terrible power. Not only may he sometimes capture a Knight, Bishop, Rook or Queen but may even checkmate the King himself!

The piece which really thoroughly enjoys forking is the Knight. His ability to leap about, attacking several pieces at once, has made the strongest players tremble.

Look at this position :

(174) White to move.
Black has a mighty Queen (worth 9 Pawns) against a Knight (worth 3 Pawns). The Queen considers her coming victory. She wonders how to smite this cheeky little warrior. But wait! He attacks! Look out, he has a lance in either hand.

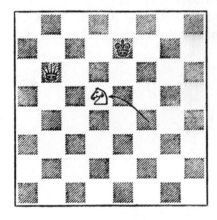

(175) The Knight fork.
The Knight moves to Q5 and has attacked the Queen and the King at the same time. Black's next move must be to get out of check. He can only move his King, leaving the Queen to be captured on White's next move.

Now we will see the Rook fork at work. The general idea is the same.

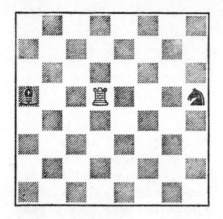

(176) In this position the Rook is attacking both Bishop and Knight. It is Black's move and as he may move only one piece to safety the other is lost.

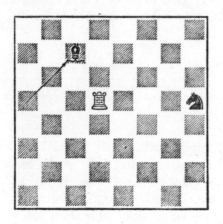

(177) Black has moved his Bishop away. White to move. The Bishop has been moved to safety but the Knight remains attacked and may be captured.

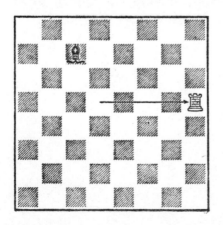

(178) R × Kt.
The Knight disappears, a victim of the fork.

(179) Here you see a Bishop fork. Only one piece can be moved, the other remains to be captured.

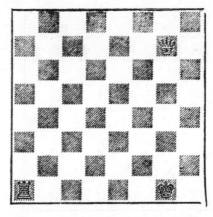

(180) A Queen fork. The King, being in check, must move and so the Rook will be captured.

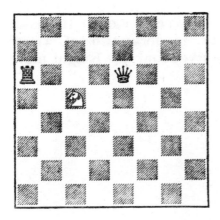

(181) Black to move. If the Queen moves, you capture the Rook. If after the capture of the Rook the Queen captures the Knight then clearly White benefits because the Rook is of more value than the Knight.

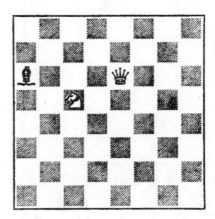

(182) If, however, you had this position instead, the fork would not be quite as strong. Black to move. After the Queen moves away, the Knight may capture the Bishop. If the Queen then recaptures the Knight the exchange is equal—both the Bishop and the Knight being worth 3 Pawns each.

(*Q.* 57) This position shows a Knight fork.
The Knight is forking two Black pieces. Can you find these two pieces which are forked ?

(*Q.* 58) It is Black's move. He has an opportunity to fork two of White's pieces. Can you find this Knight move ?

(*Q.* 59) White to move.
Using the method of double attack, can you find a way for White to win the Black Queen ? Find a double attack move, attacking the Queen.

Answers to 'Double Attack' Quiz on page 184.

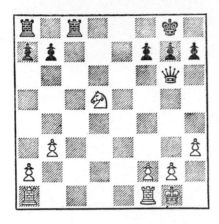

(Q. 60) Another Knight fork move to find.

This time there is a move for the White Knight which will fork *three* Black pieces at the same time. A rare chance indeed!

(Q. 61) The two Black Rooks are on the same diagonal. This spells danger! Can you find a White move attacking both these Rooks at once?

(Q. 62) The White Queen has a chance of winning the Black Bishop by a double attack move. Can you find this move?

Answers to 'Double Attack' Quiz (contd.) on page 185.

The Pin

Have you been to the Natural History Museum and seen all those wonderful insects mounted in trays ? Look closely and you will see that one way of mounting insects is to pin them to the wood underneath. No matter how carefully you examine them you will not see one leg move, nor a wing flutter nor an antenna twitch.

If you look at all three examples (diagrams 183, 184 and 185) you will see that when two enemy pieces are in a straight line, either on a rank, file or diagonal, they can be attacked by pieces that move along ranks, files or diagonals—Queen, Bishop or Rook. If the enemy piece nearest the attacker cannot move, it is said to be pinned.

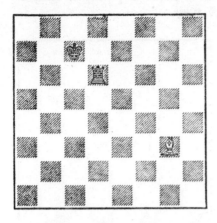

(183) The Rook here is unable to move because the King would be in check from the White Bishop. He may just as well be paralysed, or like those insects—dead ! He cannot stir from the square he is standing on. He is said to be *pinned* by the Bishop.

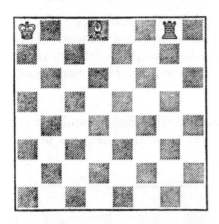

(184) It is White to move. He cannot move the Bishop because that would expose the White King to check by the Black Rook.
The White Bishop is paralysed. It is pinned.

(185) White to move.
If the Knight moved, then Black on his next move could win the Rook. The White Knight dare not move without losing the Rook, so the Knight is said to be pinned.

You can often make certain of winning this pinned piece by attacking it a second time, with another piece. Let us look at a position similar to diagram 183 but put in a White Pawn as well.

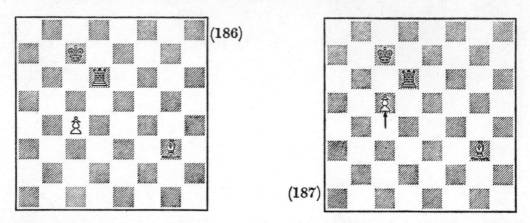

(186)

(187)

(186) White to move. He can play B×R and Black could reply K×B. White gains a piece worth 5 Pawns and loses one worth 3 Pawns. This is called winning the exchange. But by attacking the pinned Rook *twice* he can win this Rook without losing the Bishop at all. How can he do this?

(187) White plays P—B5. The Rook is pinned by the Bishop and is now attacked *again* by the saucy Pawn. While he is in this helpless state, the Pawn can gobble him up.

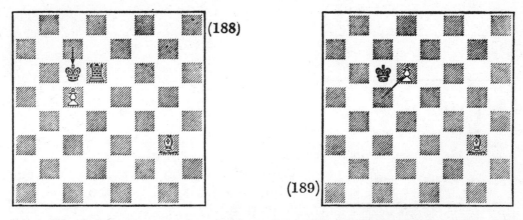

(188)

(189)

(188) Black has to move something else. He moves his King to B3.

(189) White plays P×R winning the Rook for nothing.

(*Q.* 63) Can you see which piece the White Queen is pinning ?

(*Q.* 64) It is White's move. He notices that Black has a Rook on K3 on the same diagonal as the Black King. Can he take advantage of this and *pin* the Rook ?

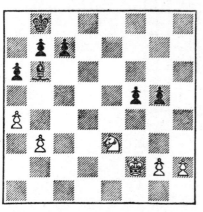

(*Q.* 65) Black to move. The White Knight is pinned by the Black Bishop. If Black plays B × Kt then White captures the Bishop with his King and the exchange is equal. Can Black take advantage of the pin with a better move ?

Answers to ' Pin ' Quiz on page 186.

Discovered Check

The Hidden Weapon

A man walks into a bank. He looks very much like any other customer. Dressed in a dark grey suit, he carries a fawn coloured mackintosh loosely slung over his right arm. He waits quietly for his turn, and then purposefully approaches the cashier behind the counter. The cashier glances up casually; but in one startling moment all the occupants of the bank are rooted to the spot. A swift movement of the man's free arm, the fawn mackintosh is whipped away and the cashier stares horror-stricken down the barrel of a menacing revolver. The moment of surprise is enough. The grey suited bandit grabs the money and is gone.

(190) It is White's move.

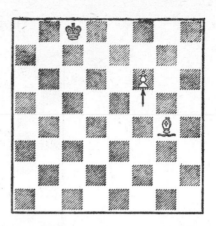

(191) White advances his Pawn P—B6. The Black King is in check by the *Bishop*. This clever move is known as *discovered check*.

(192) White's move.

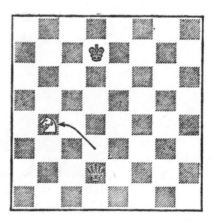

(193) White moves Kt—Kt4. There is now a clear path between the King and the attacking White Queen. The Black King is in check. The Knight, in moving, has *discovered check*.

125

Another example :

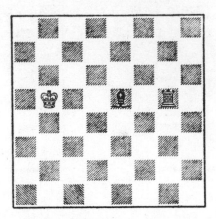

(194) Black to move.

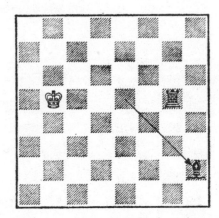

(195) Black plays B—R7. The White
King is now in check by the Black Rook.
The Bishop has *discovered check*.

You will see that the piece that moves is *not* the checking piece.
The checking piece hides behind the piece that moves. This method of
checking is known as *discovered check*.

In the next two examples (diagrams 196-199) you will see how
this cunning and dangerous move can be used to win pieces from an
opponent.

Look at this bandit Rook :

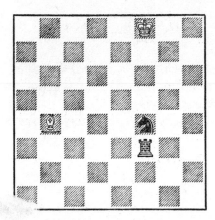

(196) The Rook is in line with the enemy White King but is hiding behind a Knight.

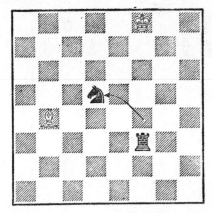

(197) . . . . . Kt—Q4. The Knight discovers check. The Rook is checking the King. All the King can do is to move away. But disaster! When the Knight moved it attacked a Bishop. After the King has moved, the Black Knight can take the Bishop.

(198) White's move. White takes advantage of the fact that the diagonal between the White Bishop and the Black King is blocked by the White Rook.

(199) White plays R—KR4 check. The King must move. White can then reply R × Q, winning the Queen.

(*Q.* 66) Black can make a move, discovering check, winning the White Queen on his next move after that.
Can you find this discovered check move ?

(*Q.* 67) This time it is White's turn. He can win the Black Queen by a discovered check move.
Can you find this move ?

(*Q.* 68) Black's turn to move. A chance to win the White Queen by a discovered check move. Can you find it ?

Answers to ' Discovered Check ' Quiz on page 187.

Mating Patterns

Suicide or Surrender

The watcher on the cliff top strains his eyes to penetrate the darkness ahead. The ringing sound of metal clashing on metal, punctuated by muffled gasps and cries, tells him that a desperate battle is in progress.

Moving cautiously forward he discerns three figures engaged in a fierce sword fight. Two men dressed in dark cloaks appear to be aiding one another ; while a third in white, desperately outnumbered, is fighting for his very life.

One dark cloaked enemy engages the White warrior from the front, the other contrives to attack from the side. Thus beset from front and flank, the single adversary is forced to move back. At each step in his retreat the couple advance apace and to the watcher it seems that in this manner the combat could go on indefinitely until the one or the others stop from sheer exhaustion. But he has reckoned without the one deciding factor—the cliff edge.

A step back—the White warrior is on the edge. A quick glance reveals the shadowy shapes of sharp rocks in the sea below. A leap would mean certain death. A sword clanks to the ground. Two dark cloaks envelop the lone fighter and he is borne off into the night.

In order to checkmate a player who is left with only his King on the board, it is necessary to have the following pieces :

a) King and Queen.
b) King and Rook.
c) King and two Bishops.
d) King, Knight and Bishop.
e) King and three Knights (this is an extremely unlikely event. Should you wonder how a player could have *three* Knights, the answer is that a Pawn may have reached the eighth rank and been promoted into a Knight).

It is clear that if a player has more pieces than required it should be easier to checkmate an opponent. In the examples that follow in this section we have left out King and two Bishops against King; King, Knight and Bishop against King; and also King and three Knights against King, as all three are most unlikely to be met by you in your games.

A King and Pawn can become a checkmating force provided you can Queen the Pawn (see diagrams 17-19, page 23).

It follows from what we have said above that if you have *fewer* pieces than required you *cannot checkmate.*

You cannot checkmate with : King and Bishop against King.
King and Knight against King.
King and two Knights against King,
except in some cases where there are other pieces on the board as well (see answer to Quiz 45, page 180).

CHECKMATE WITH KING AND QUEEN AGAINST KING

The solitary King must be driven to the side of the board.

Play the moves over on your board.

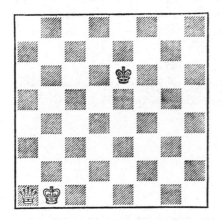

	White	Black
1.	K—B2	K—Q4
2.	K—Q3	K—B4
3.	Q—B6	K—Q4
4.	Q—K7	K—B3
5.	K—B4	K—Kt3
6.	Q—Q7	K—R3
7.	K—B5	K—R4
8.	Q—R7 or Kt5 checkmate.
(diagrams 201 and 202)

(200) The White King and Queen work together to drive the Black King back. The Black King might have moved differently but White's attack would have been similar, as would have been the final checkmating pattern. The two Kings would have one square separating them and the Queen would finally checkmate along rank or file.

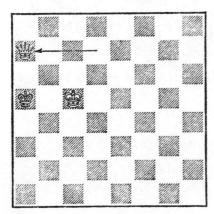

(201) 8. Q—R7 checkmate.

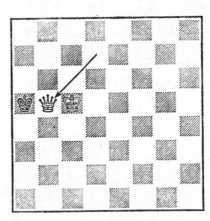

(202) or 8. Q—Kt5 checkmate.

Here is another example of checkmate by King and Queen:

(203) Black to move.

	White	Black
1.	. . . . .	K—B4
2.	K—Q5	K—Kt3
3.	Q—KB4	K—Kt2
4.	K—K6	K—Kt1
5.	K—B6	K—R1
6.	K—B7	K—R2

7. Q—KR4 or R2 checkmate.
(see diagrams 204 and 205)

(204) 7.Q—KR4 checkmate.

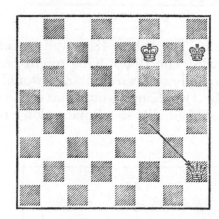

(205) or 7. Q—R2 checkmate.

The general idea is always the same:

1. Drive the King to the side.
2. Finally checkmate with the Queen.

132

Here are other checkmate positions showing King and Queen against a solitary King. There are other pieces on the board in the diagrams 206-209 but you will notice it is the Queen which does the work just as in the previous examples.

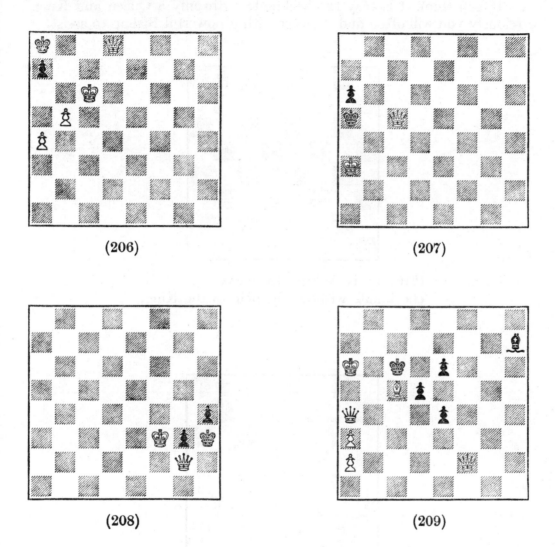

(206) (207)

(208) (209)

CHECKMATE WITH QUEEN AND BISHOP AGAINST KING

If you think it is easy to checkmate with only a Queen and King, obviously you will often find it easier with a powerful Bishop to assist.

(210) It is White to move. He can checkmate without the help of the King.

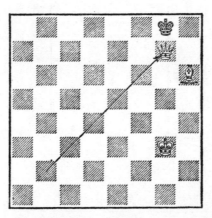

(211) The Queen moves to KKt7— checkmate !

Here are some other positions showing the Queen and Bishop checkmating. Again, in these positions you will find other pieces but it is the Queen and Bishop which finally bring the Black King to defeat.

(212)

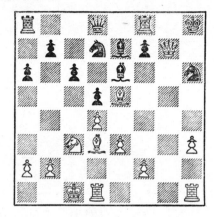

(213)

(214)

(215)

(216) In this diagram it is Black's turn to move.

(217) Black moves Q—KKt2 checkmate. Again the help of the Black King was not needed.

Here are other positions showing the Queen and Knight co-operating in checkmate.

(218)

(219)

(220)

(221)

Two Rooks may checkmate without the help of their King.

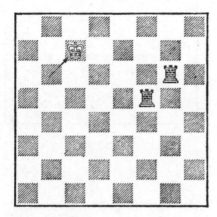

(222) K—B7.

(223) . . . . . R—B2 check.

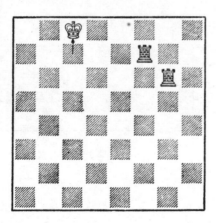

(224) K—B8.
The King has his back to the wall !

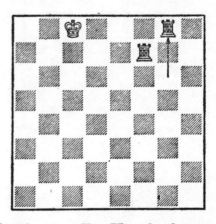

(225) . . . . . R—Kt1 checkmate.
The end has come.

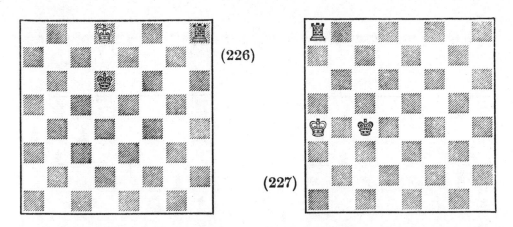

(226)

(227)

In diagrams 226 and 227 the White King is checkmated. If the White King moves out of line with the Black Rook it would move to a square next to the Black King. This, as we know, is not allowed. Two Kings must never occupy squares which are next to each other.

(228) Do you notice the difference in this position? Again the Black Rook is checking the King but this time the Black King is not directly opposite the White King. The White King is therefore able to escape.

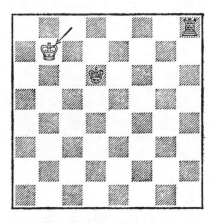

(229) The White King moves to an escape square K—Kt7.

Here are some examples showing mating patterns which often occur.

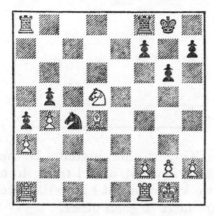

(230) Bishop and Knight work together to checkmate Black.

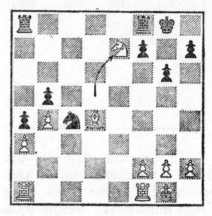

(231) One move later. White plays Kt—K7 checkmate.

(232) A Black Pawn is going to discover checkmate by the Black Bishop.

(233) . . . . . P—B7 checkmate.

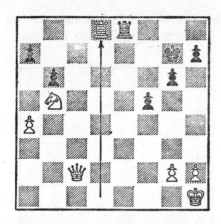

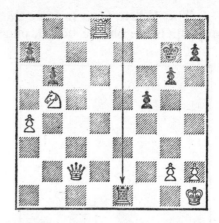

(234) Deserting his back rank, a greedy White Rook plays R×Q. The Black Queen is off the board.

(235) Punishment for White! ..... R—K8 checkmate.

141

The White Queen with the help of the Rook which commands the only open file on the board, checkmates the Black King in two moves.

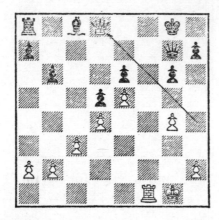

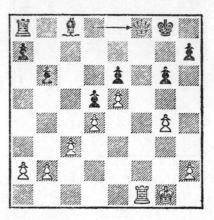

(236) 1. Q—Q8 ch. Black is forced to play 1 . . . . . Q—B1.

(237) White replies 2. Q×Q checkmate.

Black Rooks and Bishop co-operate to checkmate White in three moves.

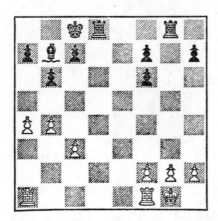

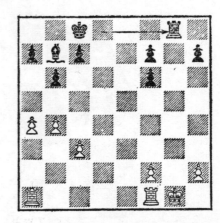

(238) In this position Black plays
1 . . . . . R×P ch.
2 K—R1 R—Kt8 double check.
3 K×R.
Both White's moves are forced.

(239) Black ends the game with 3 . . . . . . R—Kt1 checkmate.

142

Two final examples of typical checkmates.

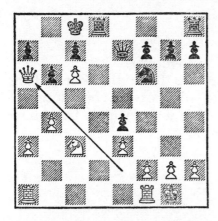

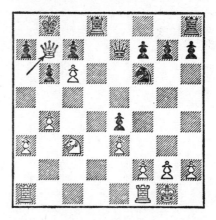

(240) White plays 1. Q—R6 check. Aided by the Pawn on B6 he will checkmate on his next move. Black's reply is forced 1 . . . . . K—Kt1.

(241) White delivers the death blow.
2. Q—Kt7 checkmate.

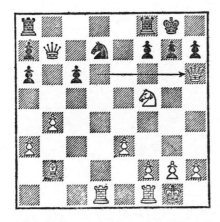

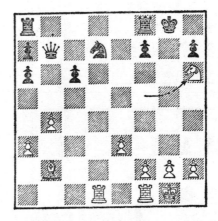

(242) White plays 1. Q—R6 threatening Q×P checkmate. Black cannot protect this Pawn on Kt2. In desperation he plays 1 . . . . . P×Q.

(243) But it is of no avail. White cuts him down.
2. Kt×P checkmate.
Notice the work of the White Bishop on QKt2, preventing Black's King moving to R1 or Kt2.

(Q. 69) White to move.
He is trying to force the Black King towards the edge of the board in the usual way. What is White's best move in this position ?

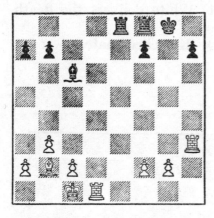

(Q. 70) White to give checkmate in one move.
Can you find this move ?

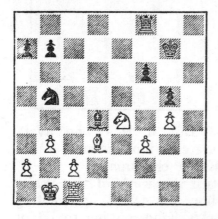

(Q. 71) Black to checkmate in one move. How can this be done ?

Answers to ' Mating Patterns ' Quiz on page 188.

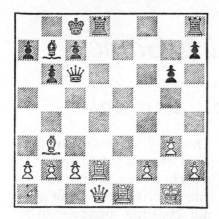

(*Q.* 72) Black to checkmate in one move.

(*Q.* 73) White to checkmate in one move.

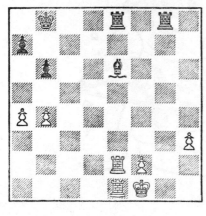

(*Q.* 74) Black to checkmate in one move.

Answers to 'Mating Patterns' Quiz (contd.) on page 189.

Winning and Drawing Games

1—HOW GAMES ARE *WON* AND *LOST*

There are two ways of winning games. One way we have learnt is to checkmate your opponent's King. The other way is as follows. It quite often happens that a player has not been checkmated, but thinks that his position is so bad that he has no chance of either winning or drawing the game. So that the game may not continue unnecessarily, this player may end the game by telling his opponent that he is giving up the struggle. In chess, there is a special way of doing this. The player *resigns*, usually laying his King down on its side and saying to his opponent—" I resign."

The two ways of winning are therefore :

    a) by checkmate,
    b) by an opponent resigning.

2—HOW GAMES ARE *DRAWN*

There are five ways of drawing games. Here they are explained simply.

(a) *too weak an army*

Both sides may continue a game until there are not sufficient pieces to checkmate. For example, only the two Kings and Bishop left on the board ; or one side may have only a King against a King—not enough to checkmate with. Similarly a King and Knight against a King would not be enough. See page 130.

(b) *by agreement*

One player may decide that the position in a game is such that a draw would be a fair result. He would say to his opponent—" I offer you a draw." If his opponent agrees to this then the game is considered drawn.

(c) *same position appearing three times*

A player or his opponent may claim a draw if the same position occurs *three* times during a game. This rule is one where you really need to study the official rules to understand it. But do not worry, this kind of position rarely happens in actual play, except when a player checks his opponent non-stop.

A position may be reached in which an opponent is unable to prevent a player from checking him after every move he makes. This situation is known as *perpetual check* and should it happen the game is drawn.

(d) *the 50 move rule*

If in the course of a game fifty moves are made by both player and his opponent, during which *no Pawn has been moved* and *no capture of a piece or Pawn has occurred* the game is drawn.

(e) *stalemate*

It is a draw when a player whose turn it is to move is unable to move and yet his King is not in check.

As perpetual check and stalemate are likely to happen quite often we are going to explain them in greater detail.

CHECKING YOUR OPPONENT NON-STOP
(*perpetual check*)

Black may claim a draw if he wishes, by saying he intends to make this kind of repeating move.

There are many other positions in which perpetual check may be possible, and very often this enables a player to draw a game he might have lost.

(244) Black plays QB—8 ch.

(245) White plays K—R2. This is the only move he may make.

(246) Black plays Q—B7 ch.

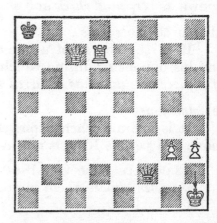

(247) White's reply is again forced. K—R1.

STALEMATE

It was cool on the fringe of the clearing and Tarna the leopard was content to lie on the downwind side. It was two days since Benson the hunter had struck the leopard's fresh trail crossing a muddy track near the river. Tarna was not unduly disturbed, for it was not the first time he had been pursued by hunters from the nearby village, anxious to put a stop to his occasional night raids on their goats.

Tarna raised his head and surveyed the scene, twitching nostrils acutely sensitive to any possible intruder. The air was hot and still and Tarna lazed drowsily.

Meanwhile Benson had moved round in a wide detour since first sighting the leopard and was now about half a mile from the clearing, approaching upwind along the dried-up course of a river bed. Benson knew he must be near the leopard and moved forward cautiously. Suddenly there was a crashing of branches in the undergrowth; and an impala, horns extended back along its graceful body, bounded across Benson's path and disappeared into the long grasses to his right. Benson cursed lightly to himself. The sound of the impala's startled dash brought Tarna to his feet, tense and expectant. The leopard and the hunter must have seen one another at the same instant, for as Benson fired Tarna bounded across the clearing, following the track that led to the nearest water hole. Benson ran swiftly in the direction of the leopard's retreat. Along the track he observed occasional spots of blood. The leopard was evidently wounded. This could be dangerous. Unexpectedly the trail swung off the track to the left towards the main river bed. Ten yards across the dried grasses was a clump of reeds, some six yards wide and twice as deep. There was no doubt Tarna was there. Benson stopped with his back to a nearby tree and surveyed the scene. To enter the reeds would almost certainly be fatal. He would have to wait.

Tarna was angry. He lay still, his flank smarting where Benson's bullet had ploughed a six-inch long groove. There was no choice but to stay where he was. Tarna could see Benson clearly, though the latter was unable to observe the leopard in the innermost gloom of the reeds. Hunter and hunted waited motionless. It was stalemate.

Swiftly the tropical twilight enveloped the scene. Benson turned homewards. The conflict would have to be renewed another day.

A peculiar situation arises sometimes when a player whose turn it is to move finds he is unable to do so and yet he is *not* in check. This is a strange situation indeed and is called STALEMATE. The game is over. The result is a *DRAW*.

We know that if you attack your opponent's King and he cannot get out of check, then it is checkmate. But in the case of stalemate the King is not in check and still your opponent cannot move.

Look at this position :

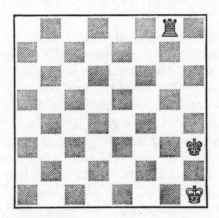

(248) It is White's turn to move. He is not permitted to move his King because by doing so he would either be moving into check or next to his opponent's King, and neither as we know, is allowed. It would be an illegal move. He is not in check at the moment, so we cannot call it checkmate. The position is STALEMATE and the game is drawn.

It is only stalemate if, while not in check, you cannot move any piece anywhere on the chessboard.

Here is another example :

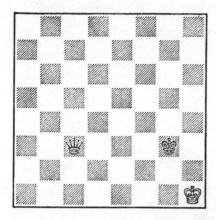

(249) In this position Black is going to move. If he is careless he can stalemate his opponent and turn a game he could win into a draw.

(250) Black plays Q—K6. A very poor move for now the White King is in a position of stalemate. He is not in check and yet cannot move to any square.

Two more stalemate positions :

(251) Black to move. He finds he cannot—stalemate !

(252) White to move. Stalemate again ! It is very easy to bring about stalemate when there is a King and Queen against King. Take care to avoid this.

(253) White's turn to move. The White Pawn is blocked by Black's Pawn and so cannot move. The White King is not in check but there is no square to which it is allowed to move. There being no other piece that White can move, this is again a stalemate position.

(254) Black to move. You will see that the Black King cannot move. Both the empty squares next to this King are attacked by the White Rook. The Black King is not in check. Is this stalemate? No! For the Black Player has *other* pieces on the board which can move. He may move either his Pawn or Knight.

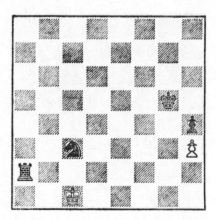

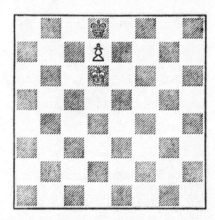

(255) White to move. Here again White has a blocked Pawn and the King not in check. With no square for the King to go to, this is another stalemate position.

(256) Black to move. White has been trying to Queen his Pawn and win. The game is drawn, however, as Black is unable to move—stalemate!

(*Q. 75*) White has just played **Q—K7**. It is Black's turn now. Can Black move ?

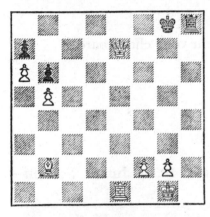

(*Q. 76*) White has just played **Q—K7**. This could be a drawn game. How ?

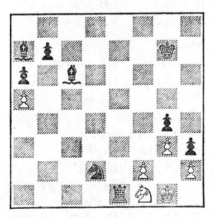

(*Q. 77*) Black has just played **Kt—Q7**. Can you see why this is not a good move ?

Answers to 'Stalemate' Quiz on page **190**.

Games with Comment

In the games which follow we have made remarks to help you to see the kinds of moves we have been talking about. The first three games which we have chosen for this purpose were played by children under fourteen. The final game we show was played between A. Niemzowitch and S. Alapin in a chessmasters' tournament in 1911.

You should play these games over on your chessboard.

GAME No. 3

Played in the London Boys' Championships, 1956, Junior Section—under 14.

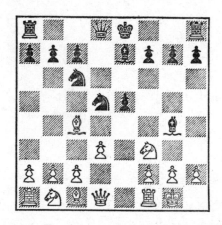

(257) Position after Black's 8th move . . . . . B—KKt5.

	White	Black
	R. OXENHAM	M. SHAW
1.	P—K4	P—K4
2.	Kt—KB3	Kt—QB3
3.	B—B4	B—B4
4.	P—Q3	Kt—B3

Both players have developed their pieces well.

| 5. | Kt—Kt5 | P—Q4 |
| 6. | P×P | Kt×P |

Exchanging Pawn for Pawn.

| 7. | O—O | B—K2 |

The White Knight

154

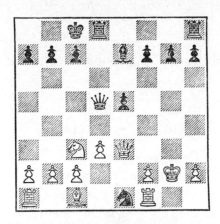

(258) Position after Black's 15th move . . . . . Kt—K8 ch.

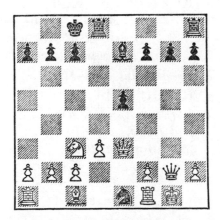

(259) Position after Black's 16th move . . . . . Q—Kt7 mate.

on Kt5 is now attacked twice, by Q and B, and defended only by White Bishop on QB1.

8. Kt—KB3
The Knight retreats, allowing the Black Bishop to pin it.
. . . . . B—KKt5
Pinning the Knight. If the Knight moves the Queen is lost. (See diagram 257)

9. Q—K1   B×Kt
Exchanging Bishop for Knight

10. P×B   Q—Q3
11. B×Kt   Q×B
12. Q—K2   O—O—O
13. Kt—B3
Attacking Queen
. . . . Kt—Q5
Black replies by attacking White's Queen with his Knight.

14. Q—K3   Kt×P check.
15. K—Kt2   Kt—K8 check !
In moving, the Knight has discovered check by the Queen. So this is an example of Double Check. (See diagram 258)

16. K—Kt1   Q—Kt7 mate
(See diagram 259)

155

Played in the London Boys' Championships, 1956, Junior Section—under 14.

(260) Position after White's 8th move Kt—B7 check.

(261) Position after White's 9th move Kt×Q check.

White	Black
L. CHIN	S. NAYLER

1. P—K4   P—K4
2. Kt—KB3   Q—KB3

A poor move. The Queen soon becomes a target.

3. B—B4   **B—B4**
4. Kt—B3

White rightly continues to develop his pieces in contrast with Black's next move.

..... P—KKt4

5. Kt—Q5

Attacking Queen.

..... Q—Q3

6. Kt×KtP   P—KB3

Allows White to check at R5, with disastrous results.

7. Q—R5 ch.   K—Q1
8. Kt—B7 ch. !

Forking King, Queen and Rook.
(See diagram 260)

..... K—K1

This move forced.

9. Kt×Q check.

In moving, the Knight has discovered check with the Queen. So this

(262) Position after White's 10th move Q—B7 mate.

is another example of
Double Check.
(See diagram 261)
        .....K—B1
10. Q—B7 mate.
    (See diagram 262)

GAME No. 5

Played in the London Boys' Championships, 1956, Junior Section—under 14.

White	Black
R. OXENHAM	J. JORDAN

1. P—K4   P—QB4
2. Kt—KB3   Kt—KB3
3. Kt—B3   P—Q3
4. B—B4   B—Kt5
               *Pinning the
               King's Kt.*
5. P—KR3
   *White prepares to
   drive the Bishop
   away.*
        .....B—R4
6. P—KKt4   B—Kt3
7. P—K5   Kt—K5
8. P—Q3
   (See diagram 263)

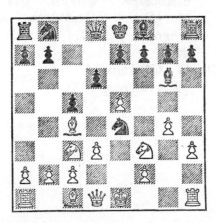

(263) Position after White's 8th move P—Q3.

157

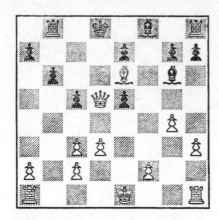

(264) Position after White's 18th move B—K6 check.

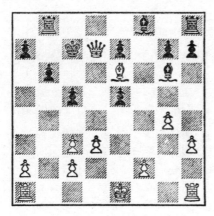

(265) Position after White's 19th move Q—Q7 mate.

8 . . . .   Kt×Kt

To avoid capture by the Pawn, Black exchanges Knights.

9. P×Kt   Kt—B3
10. B—B4   P×P
11. Kt×P   Kt×Kt
12. B×Kt   P—B3
13. Q—Kt1   P×B
14. Q—Kt3   P—Kt3
15. B—Kt5 check !

Winning the Queen.

. . . . . Q—Q2

Black is forced to play this move. The King cannot escape to KB2 as this square is attacked by the White Queen.

16. B×Q ch.   K—Q1
17. Q—Q5   R—QKt1
18. B—K6 ch.   K—B2

Good example of discovered ch. (See diagram 264).   *If Black had played K—K1, Queen still checkmates at Q7.*

19. Q—Q7 mate
(*See diagram 265*)

158

MASTER CHESS

This final game was played in the Carlsbad Tournament, 1911. The standard of play shown here is high; in fact it is the play of chess-masters. For this reason it is unlikely that you will understand the purpose for all the moves. We have included this example, however, firstly to give you an idea what 'master' chess is like and secondly in the hope that one day You will become a chessmaster, in which case you will be able to play this game over the board and learn ALL its secrets!

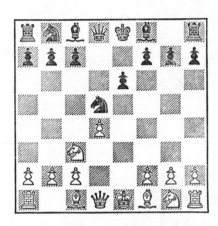

(266) Position after Black's 4th move .... Kt×P.

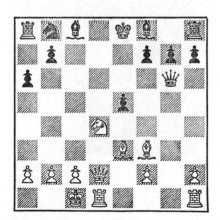

(267) Position after White's 12th move O—O—O.

GAME No. 6

White	Black
A. NIEMZOWITCH	S. ALAPIN

1.	P—K4	P—K3
2.	P—Q4	P—Q4
3.	Kt—QB3	Kt—KB3
4.	P×P	Kt×P
		(See diagram 266)
5.	Kt—B3	P—QB4
6.	Kt×Kt	Q×Kt
7.	B—K3	P×P
8.	Kt×P	P—QR3
9.	B—K2	Q×KtP
10.	B—B3	Q—Kt3
11.	Q—Q2	P—K4
12.	O—O—O	P×Kt
		(See diagram 267)
13.	B×QP	Kt—B3
14.	B—B6	Q×B
15.	KR—K1ch.	B—K2
16.	B×Ktch.	K—B1
17.	Q—Q8ch.	B×Q
18.	R—K8 mate	
		(See diagram 268 on next page)

159

(268) Position after White's 18th move R—K8 mate.

(*See page* **159** *for rest of Game No. 6*)

160

Some Items of Interest

THE INVENTION OF CHESS

Jane Brown was eight and a bright girl for her age. Mr. Brown had just finished giving his daughter her first chess lesson.

They sat by the fire. Mr. Brown lit his pipe and picked up his newspaper once more. Jane stared into the heart of the fire, where flames flickered and escaping gas hissed, bursting into bright yellow jets of flame amid the glowing coals.

" How did it all start, Dad ? "

The newspaper was lowered. " All what, Jane ? "

" Why chess of course ! "

Mr. Brown frowned. Yes, how did it all start ? That was some question. He relit his pipe. The flame of the match curled inwards, disappearing into the bowl, and a succession of grey smoke puffs ascended, hiding from Jane's earnest gaze the twinkle that had appeared in Mr. Brown's eyes.

" Many, many centuries ago there was a King who lived in a lonely palace. Because of this and surrounded as he was by the same palace servants, with few visitors, the King became bored. To overcome his boredom he employed a Master of Games. This man was extremely inventive and the King was well amused by the various games he devised for the royal pleasure.

" One day the King sent for him and said, ' I wish for a game that will surpass all that you have invented for me so that I may never have a dull moment again.'

" The Master of Games departed and in three days returned to the palace. Summoned before the King he unwrapped the parcel he carried. He opened before him a square board covered with sixty-four squares in black and white and upon these placed thirty-two wooden figures. The King was eager to start and listened impatiently as the Master of Games explained the method of play. From that moment on, the King never left his chessboard. Having taught the palace servants to play and defeated them all, he took to inviting passing village folk to play. It must be admitted that his ability to win all the time was due to the fact that he did not hesitate to alter the rules when it suited him. But for all that he was no longer bored. In fact, so delighted was he with his new pastime that once more he sent for his Master of Games.

" ' Whatever you would care to ask of me for a gift is yours,' said the King. The Master of Games thought for a moment and then replied.

" ' Your Majesty is indeed very generous, but my request is a small one. All I ask for is the number of grains of wheat which can be arrived at in this wise :

" ' One grain of wheat for the first square, two grains for the second, four grains for the third, eight grains for the fourth, sixteen grains next, then thirty-two and so on."

" ' A few grains of wheat ! Is that all for such a wondrous game ? '

" ' That is all I ask, your Majesty,' replied the Master of Games.

" The King sent for his mathematician. He was not much good at Arithmetic himself. He told him of the Master of Games' request. The mathematician shrugged his shoulders in bewilderment and departed. It was many hours before he returned. Consternation was upon his face.

" 'Speak up man, speak up,' demanded the King, banging a Pawn down on the board so hard that all the other thirty-one pieces jumped up and down.

" ' Sire, I began the calculation 2, 4, 8, 16, 32, 64, 128, 256, 512, 1024 . . .'

" ' Yes, yes, go on, go on.'

" ' That's just it, your Majesty, I went on for sixty-four squares, as you said and the number becomes . . .

" ' 9,223,372,036,854,775,808. That is more wheat than we have in the entire Kingdom ! ' "

The Master of Games had invented his last game.

CHESS CLUBS

Not very far from where you live there is bound to be a Chess Club of some sort. We suggest that when your school studies permit, or when you have left school (certainly not before you are a teenager) you should get in touch with your nearest Chess Club. Whether you are a strong or a weak player or even if you are a ' learner ' you will find others in the club just like you. Once you have been a member of a club for a few weeks you will find your play improve by leaps and bounds. All the best Chess Clubs have reduced subscription rates for their younger members.

162

YOU THINK YOU ARE TOO YOUNG
TO PLAY CHESS?

Sammy Reshevsky was eight years of age when he began touring in America and Europe playing the strongest chess players. He was so clever that he often played many of these *at once*. On one occasion Sammy and his manager were met at a railway station by an American chessmaster named Edward Lasker. Lasker told Sammy he would call a taxi to take them to the hotel and suggested that on the way they look at the interesting sights. Sammy was not interested in the sights, and asked Lasker if he could play chess without using a chessboard at all! Lasker said he could, so Sammy demanded that they begin a game there and then.* As soon as they arrived at the hotel Sammy rushed into the bedroom, flung himself on the bed and continued playing the game of chess. Eventually Lasker managed to gain the upper hand in the game. Suddenly Sammy jumped up and said, " I'm hungry now. Let's go and find a restaurant where I can eat."

* This is called blindfold chess. In blindfold chess you do not use a blindfold ! The idea is to play without looking at the board.

CHESS CHAMPIONS

If you should find yourself beating all-comers on the chessboard, you may one day enter for one of the big championships. Chessmasters from all over the world compete, and hundreds of spectators are able to follow the games either by watching the actual boards of play, or large wall diagrams which show the positions of the games move by move. The title of Chessmaster is bestowed only after skill of a very high order has been reached.

Great names of the chess world include the following : Anderssen, Staunton, Morphy, Steinitz, Lasker, Capablanca, Alekhine, Euwe, M. Botvinnik and Bobby Fischer.

CHESS CLOCKS

Not very long ago there was no such thing as a chess clock, and even when playing a most important tournament game the opponents were allowed to take as much time over a move as they liked. Sometimes a player would take hours over one move, and a game might go on for more than 15 hours! This made it difficult to organise tournaments.

Chess clocks were introduced to ensure that games are completed in a reasonable time. They are used mainly in matches. Each player has to make a certain number of moves in a given time. If a player fails to do this he loses the game.

The chess clock is really two clocks connected together. It is rather like having two stop watches, one for the player with the White pieces, and one for the player with the Black pieces. When it is the White player's turn to move, his clock is started. As soon as he has made his move he presses a lever which stops his clock, at the same time starting Black's clock. Black's clock will continue to go until he has made his move, when he will press his lever in a similar way, stopping his clock and starting his opponent's. And so it will go on.

THE RULES OF CHESS

All the chess federations of the world are members of the Fédération Internationale des Échecs (The International Chess Federation—sometimes known as F.I.D.E.). This organisation lays down the rules of the game. The British Chess Federation has produced a small booklet called 'The Laws of Chess.' If you are particularly keen you may like to buy a copy. We have not explained every rule of the game in this book, but all the rules are to be found in 'The Laws of Chess,' published in an inexpensive edition by Sir Isaac Pitman & Sons, Ltd.

Answers to Quiz Questions

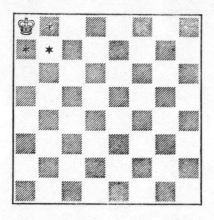

(*Q.* 1) The King can move to any of the three squares marked **.**

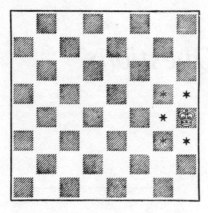

(*Q.* 2) The King can move to any of the five squares marked. *

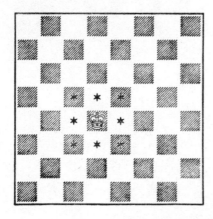

(*Q.* 3) The King can move to any of the eight squares marked **.**

'*King*' *Quiz appears on page* 20.

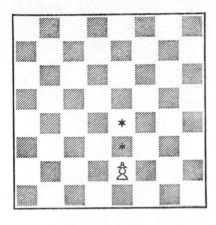

(*Q. 4*) The Pawn can move to either of the two squares marked *.

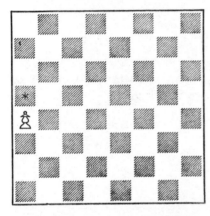

(*Q. 5*) The Pawn can move only to the square marked *.

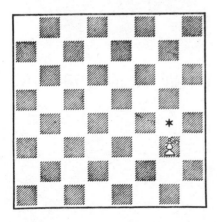

(*Q. 6*) The Pawn can move only to the square marked *.

'Pawn' Quiz appears on page 24.

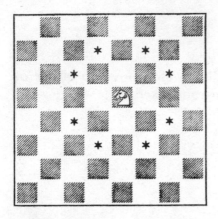

(*Q.* 7) The Knight can move to any of the eight squares marked *.

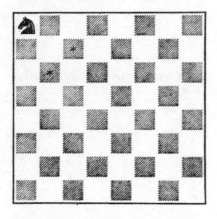

(*Q.* 8) The Knight can move to either of the two squares marked *.

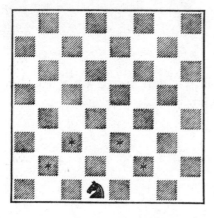

(*Q.* 9) The Knight can move to any of the four squares marked *.

'Knight' Quiz appears on page 28.

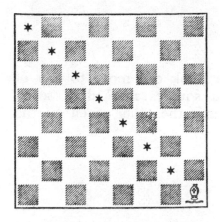

(*Q.* 10) The Bishop can move to any of the seven squares along the diagonal marked *.

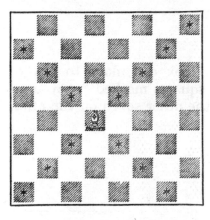

(*Q.* 11) The Bishop can move to any of the thirteen squares marked * along the two diagonals.

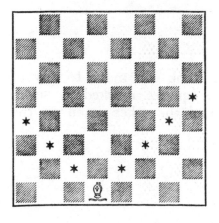

(*Q.* 12) The Bishop can move to any of the seven squares marked * along the two diagonals.

'Bishop' Quiz appears on page 31.

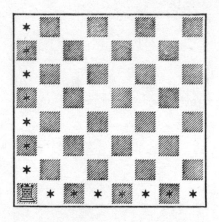

(*Q.* 13) The Rook can move to any of the fourteen squares marked *, seven on the file and the other seven on the rank.

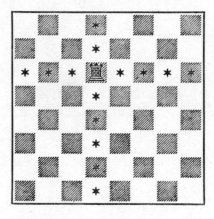

(*Q.* 14) The Rook can move to any of the fourteen squares marked *, seven on the file and the other seven on the rank.

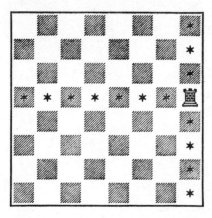

(*Q.* 15) The Rook can move to any of the fourteen squares marked *, seven on the file and the other seven on the rank.

'Rook' Quiz appears on page 34.

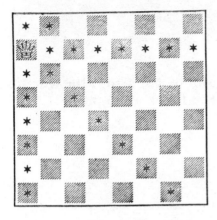

(Q. 16) The Queen can move to any of the twenty-one squares marked *. Seven appear on the file, seven on the rank and the remaining seven diagonally.

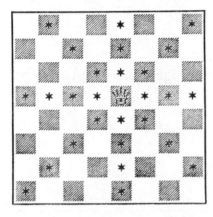

(Q. 17) The Queen can move to any of the twenty-seven squares marked *. Seven appear on the file, seven on the rank and the remaining thirteen diagonally.

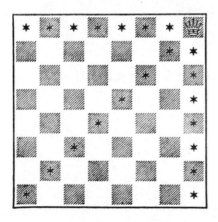

(Q. 18) The Queen can move to any of the twenty-one squares marked *. Seven appear on the file, seven on the rank and the remaining seven diagonally.

Queen Quiz appears on page 37.

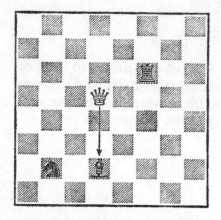

(Q. 19) As shown by the arrow, the Queen can capture the Black Bishop.

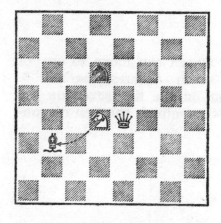

(Q. 20) The **Knight** can capture the Bishop.

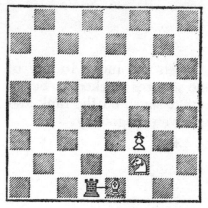

(Q. 21) The Rook is attacking the White Bishop.

' Capturing ' Quiz appears on page 45.

ANSWERS TO 'MOVING AWAY FROM ATTACK' QUIZ

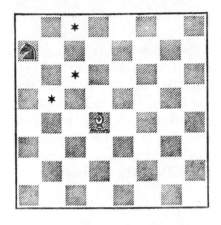

(Q. 22) The Knight can escape capture by moving to any of the three squares marked *.

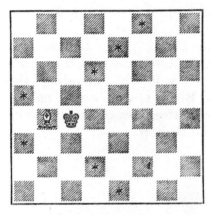

(Q. 23) Because the King can only move *one* square at a time, the White Bishop does not have to move very far before it finds an escape square. There are seven escape squares in this position, marked *.

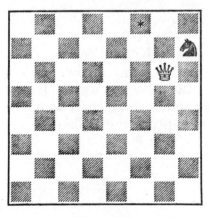

(Q. 24) The Black Knight has *one* square to which it can move without being taken by the White Queen on the following move. It is marked *.

' Moving Away from Attack ' Quiz appears on page 49.

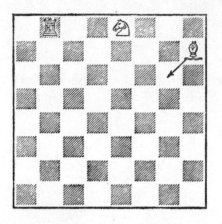

(*Q.* 25) The White Bishop can move to the square shown by the arrow. Then if the Rook were to take the Knight, the Rook would be taken by the Bishop. It would not be worth losing a Rook (worth 5 Pawns) for the sake of winning a Knight (worth 3 Pawns). Thus the Knight is defended by the Bishop.

(*Q.* 26) If the Pawn moves two squares forward (which it may do as this is its *first* move) it will be defending the Bishop. The Black Queen would not be likely to throw itself away for the sake of winning the Bishop.

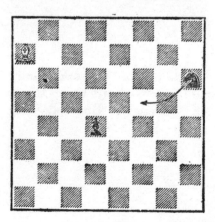

(*Q.* 27) The Black Knight can move to the square shown by the arrow. It will then defend the Black Pawn. If the White Bishop should take the Pawn, the Knight would capture the Bishop.

'Defending the Attacked Piece' Quiz appears on page 53.

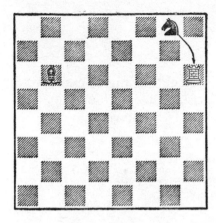

(*Q.* 28) Yes. Black's Knight can capture the White Rook.

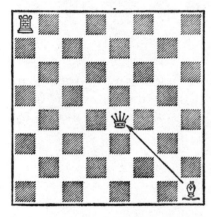

(*Q.* 29) Yes. White's Bishop is on the same diagonal as the Black Queen, and so can capture it.

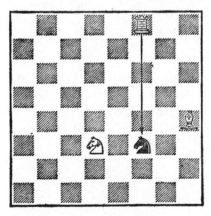

(*Q.* 30) Yes. White's Rook can capture the Knight.

'Capturing the Attacker' Quiz appears on page 57.

(*Q. 31*) Yes. Black's Knight can move in front of the Queen, blocking the attack, as shown by the arrow.

(*Q. 32*) Yes. Black's Knight moves in front of the Queen protecting it from the White Rook's attack, as shown by the arrow.

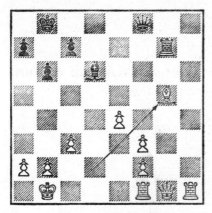

(*Q. 33*) White can move his Bishop, as shown by the arrow, blocking the Black Rook's attack on the Queen.

'Moving a Piece in the Way' Quiz appears on page 60.

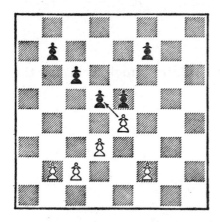

(*Q.* 34) The White Pawn, as shown by the arrow, can capture the Black Pawn.

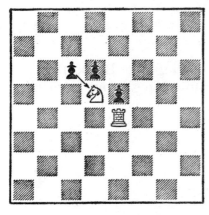

(*Q.* 35) The Black Pawn, as shown by the arrow, can capture the White Knight.

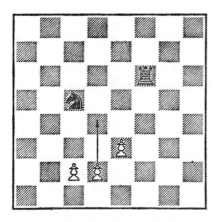

(*Q.* 36) As shown by the arrow, this White Pawn can make a move two squares forward, attacking the Black Knight.

' Attacking and Capturing with Pawns' Quiz appears on page 66.

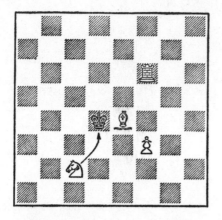

(*Q.* 37) The White Knight checks the Black King.

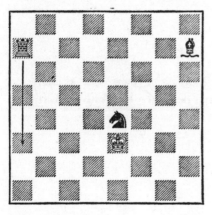

(*Q.* 38) By moving the Black Rook as shown, the White King is put in check.

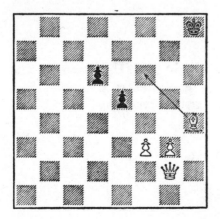

(*Q.* 39) White moves his Bishop, as shown, checking the Black King.

'Check' Quiz appears on page 75.

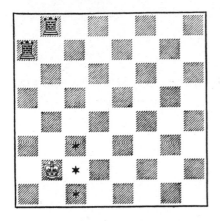

(Q. 40) The White King can move to any one of the three squares marked *.

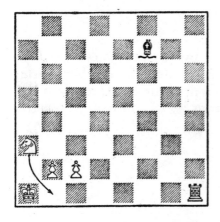

(Q. 41) The White King cannot move out of check. The Black Bishop prevents him moving forward one square.
But the White Knight can move back and cover the King from the Rook's attack, as shown by the arrow.

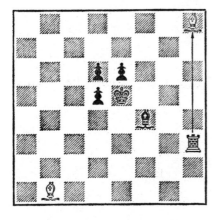

(Q. 42) The King cannot move, but the Rook can capture the Bishop, as shown by the arrow.

' Getting out of Check ' Quiz appears on page 76.

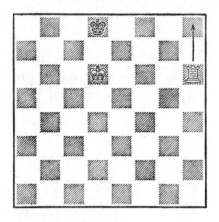

(*Q.* 43) White moves his Rook as shown. The Black King being on the edge of the board is checkmated.

(*Q.* 44) Black moves the Queen next to the White King and it is checkmate. There is no escape, for the Queen cannot be captured as it is protected by the Bishop.

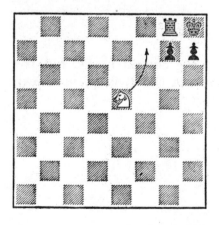

(*Q.* 45) The White Knight can checkmate as shown.

' Checkmate' Quiz appears on page 80.

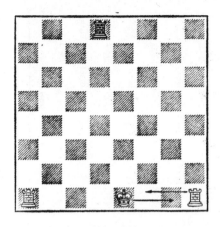

(*Q.* 46) White is prevented from castling on the Queen's side of the board, by the Black Rook. To do so would mean the King crossing a square attacked by an enemy piece—the Black Rook. But White is free to castle on the other side, as shown.

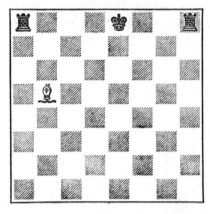

(*Q.* 47) No! The King is in check. Black is therefore not allowed to castle on his next move.

(*Q.* 48) Can you see that both the White squares on either side of the White King are attacked by the Black Queen? Whichever side White chose to castle it would mean the King crossing one of those attacked squares. The Black Queen is therefore preventing castling on *both* sides of the board in this position.

'Castling' Quiz appears on page 87.

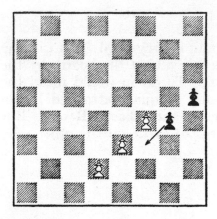

(*Q.* 49) Yes. Black can take as shown by the arrow.

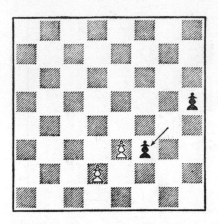

Position after the Black Pawn has taken the White Pawn from the board.

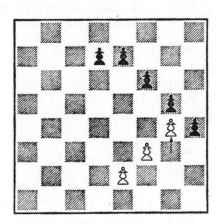

(*Q.* 50) No. Although the White Pawn has moved alongside the Black Pawn, it has moved forward only *one* square, not two.

' *En Passant* ' *Quiz appears on page* 97.

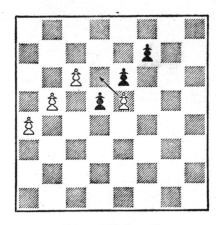

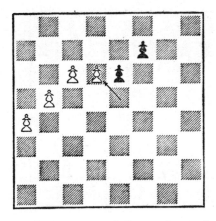

(Q. 51) The White Pawn can capture as shown.

Here is the position after the capture.

ANSWERS TO 'NOTATION' QUIZ

Quiz 52	P—B5	There is no need to say QB5, as there is a Pawn on KB5 already so no Pawn could move there.
Quiz 53	Kt—KR4	Here we must say which R4, as it is possible for the other Knight to move to QR4.
Quiz 54	R—B6	No need to say which B6 square, as the Rook can only move to this one.
Quiz 55	P×P	No need to say which Pawn takes which, as only one Pawn capture is possible.
Quiz 56	B—K2	We hope you remembered to count the squares from Black's side of the board.

'*Notation*' *Quiz appears on pages* 110 *and* 111.

(*Q.* 57) The Knight has forked both Black Queen and Black Rook.

(*Q.* 58) . . . . Kt—Q5 forking White Bishop and White Queen.

(*Q.* 59) R—Q8 ch.
If the Black King moves away, then the White Rook can remove the Black Queen.
Best move for Black would be to capture the checking Rook with his Queen, but even then he loses his Queen next move. White takes the Black Queen with his other Rook on Q1.

' Double Attack ' Quiz appears on page 118.

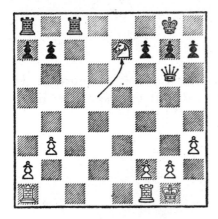

(*Q.* 60) Kt—K7 ch.
Forking King, Queen and Rook.

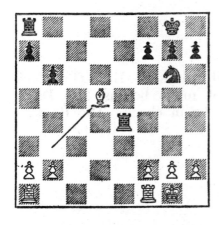

(*Q.* 61) B—Q5.

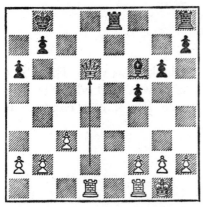

(*Q.* 62) Q—Q6 ch.
The King must move and then White
plays Q×B.

' *Double Attack* ' **Quiz** (*contd.*) *appears on page* 119.

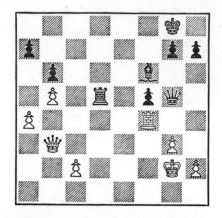

(Q. 63) The Black Rook is pinned. It cannot move without exposing the King to check by the White Queen.

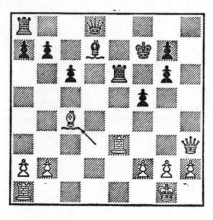

(Q. 64) White plays B—B4. The Black Rook cannot move because the Black King would be in check. The Rook is pinned.

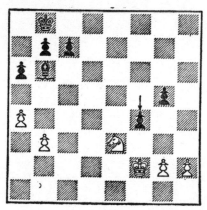

(Q. 65) Yes. Black plays P—B5. The White Knight is now attacked twice and on his next move Black can capture it without loss.

'Pin' Quiz appears on page 123.

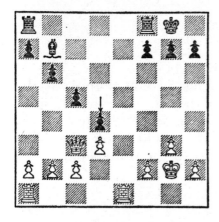

(Q. 66) . . . P—Q5 ch.
The White King is now in check from the Black Bishop, and the White Queen is attacked by the Pawn. However White replies, the White Queen is lost.

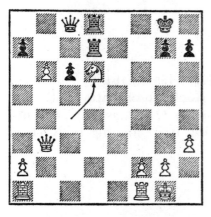

(Q. 67) Kt—Q6 ch.
The Black King is now exposed to check from the White Queen. At the same time the Black Queen is under attack. Black must deal with the check first and thus will lose his Queen.

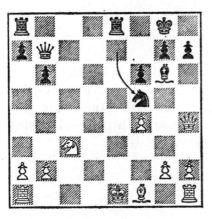

(Q. 68) . . . . Kt—B4 ch.
The White King is under check from the Black Rook on K1, and also the Black Knight attacks the White Queen. The Queen is thus lost.

' Discovered Check ' Quiz appears on page 128.

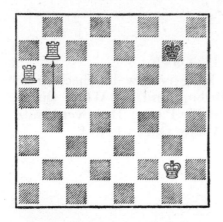

(*Q.* 69) R—Kt7 ch.
The Black King is now forced to the edge of the board. It would have been wrong to move the other Rook. R—R7ch. This would allow the King to slip back on to the third rank.

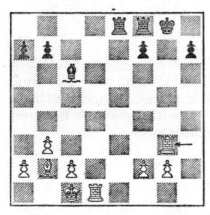

(*Q.* 70) R—Kt3 checkmate.
The White Rook co-operates with the White Bishop on QKt2, which prevents the Black King from moving to KR1.

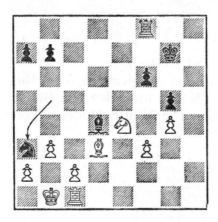

(*Q.* 71) . . . . Kt—R6 checkmate.
The Black Bishop on Q5 prevents K—R1 or Kt2. . . . . Kt—B6 would not give checkmate because White could play Kt×Kt, or move his King.

' Mating Patterns ' Quiz appears on page **144**.

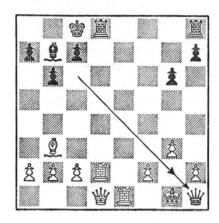

(Q. 72) .... Q—R8 or Kt7 checkmate.

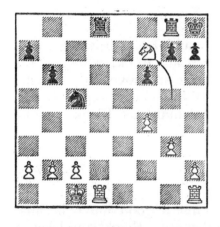

(Q. 73) Kt—B7 checkmate.

(Q. 74) .... B×P checkmate.
The Black Rook on Kt1 assists the Bishop because it controls an open file.

' Mating Patterns ' Quiz (*contd.*) *appears on page 145.*

(*Q.* 75) No. Black's Pawns may not move as they are blocked by White's Pawns. Black's King cannot move to KR1 as this is attacked by the White Bishop. The remaining four squares next to the King are also attacked. It is stalemate.

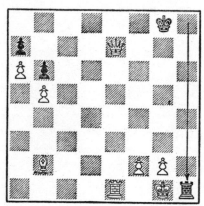

(*Q.* 76) This could be a drawn game if Black sacrifices his Rook, which is the only piece he can move, by playing R—R8 ch. White *must* reply K × R. It is then stalemate as Black has no move left.

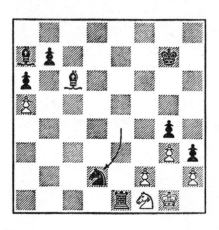

(*Q.* 77) It is not a good move because it is now stalemate. Black could easily have won if he had played a better move. The empty squares next to the White King are attacked by a Black Bishop at B3, so clearly the King cannot move. The White Knight cannot move because this would discover check by the Black Rook on K8. The White Pawn on B2 cannot move as this would discover check by the Black Bishop on R2. The remaining three White Pawns are blocked by Black Pawns.

' Stalemate ' Quiz appears on page 153.

Dictionary of Chess Terms

Check	When the King's square is attacked by an opponent's piece.
Checkmate	When a King cannot escape from check.
Defend	To protect, guard or support a piece against an attack.
Development	Bringing pieces on to squares where they are more active.
Discovered Check	A position in which one piece has moved to uncover check by another piece.
Double Attack	Two pieces attacked at the same time.
Double Check	A position in which a King is in check from *two* pieces at once.
En passant	A special kind of Pawn capturing move.
En prise	A piece is said to be " en prise " when it is being attacked.
Exchange	A series of moves in which each side captures pieces.
Forced Move	No other move is possible.
Fork	A particular type of double attack.
Gambit	An opening where a piece (usually a Pawn) is given up, with the idea of gaining an advantage later on in the game.
Illegal Move	A move that is not allowed. One that breaks the rules of the game.
J'adoube	Spoken by players when they wish to make it clear that they are not making a move but merely standing a piece correctly on its square.

Minor piece	A Bishop or a Knight.
Open File	A file on which there are no Pawns.
Opening	The first few moves of a game.
Passed Pawn	A Pawn which has no opponent's Pawn in front of it on its own file, and which in moving to the 8th rank does not have to pass an opponent's Pawn on either of the adjoining two files.
Pin	A piece is pinned when it cannot move without exposing another piece to attack.
!	Used in notation to indicate a good move (for example B—Kt5!).
?	Used in notation to indicate a bad move (for example Q—R4?).